Donna Dewberry's
PAINTED garden

Donna Dewberry's
PAINTED *garden*

NORTH LIGHT BOOKS
CINCINNATI, OHIO
WWW.ARTISTSNETWORK.COM

DONNA DEWBERRY'S PAINTED GARDEN Copyright © 2007 by Donna Dewberry. Manufactured in China. All rights reserved. No part of this book may be reproduced in any form or by any electronic or mechanical means including information storage and retrieval systems without permission in writing from the publisher, except by a reviewer who may quote brief passages in a review. The content of this book has been thoroughly reviewed for accuracy. However, the author and publisher disclaim any liability for any damages, losses or injuries that may result from the use or misuse of any product or information presented herein. It is the purchaser's responsibility to read and follow all instructions and warnings on all product labels. Published by North Light Books, an imprint of F+W Publications, Inc., 4700 East Galbraith Road, Cincinnati, Ohio, 45236. (800) 289-0963. First Edition.

Other fine North Light Books are available from your local bookstore, art supply store or direct from the publisher.

11   10   09   08   07   5   4   3   2   1

DISTRIBUTED IN CANADA BY FRASER DIRECT
100 Armstrong Avenue
Georgetown, ON, Canada L7G 5S4
Tel: (905) 877-4411

DISTRIBUTED IN THE U.K. AND EUROPE BY DAVID & CHARLES
Brunel House, Newton Abbot, Devon, TQ12 4PU, England
Tel: (+44) 1626 323200, Fax: (+44) 1626 323319
Email: postmaster@davidandcharles.co.uk

DISTRIBUTED IN AUSTRALIA BY CAPRICORN LINK
P.O. Box 704, S. Windsor NSW, 2756 Australia
Tel: (02) 4577-3555

LIBRARY OF CONGRESS CATALOGING-IN-PUBLICATION DATA
Dewberry, Donna S.
    Donna Dewberry's painted garden / Donna Dewberry.
            p. cm
    Includes index.
    ISBN-13: 978-1-58180-948-0 (hardcover : alk. paper)
    ISBN-10: 1-58180-948-4 (hardcover : alk. paper)
    ISBN-13: 978-1-58180-949-7 (pbk. : alk. paper)
    ISBN-10: 1-58180-949-2 (pbk. : alk. paper)
  1. Painting. 2. Decoration and ornament. 3. Garden ornaments and furniture. I. Title.
TT385.D48422 2007
745.7'23—dc22
                              2006037848

Edited by Kathy Kipp
Designed by Clare Finney
Interior Layout by Kathy Gardner
Production coordinated by Greg Nock
Photographed by Christine Polomsky and Tim Grondin

METRIC CONVERSTION CHART

To convert	to	multiply by
Inches	Centimeters	2.54
Centimeters	Inches	0.4
Feet	Centimeters	30.5
Centimeters	Feet	0.03
Yards	Meters	0.9
Meters	Yards	1.1

ABOUT THE AUTHOR

Donna Dewberry is the most successful decorative painter ever. She is the originator of the One-Stroke painting technique, and has developed the One-Stroke Certified Instructor (OSCI) program for teachers. She is seen weekly on PBS stations nationwide with her program "One-Stroke Painting with Donna Dewberry" and is also a regular presenter on the Home Shopping Network and America's Store. Her designs are licensed for home décor fabrics, wallpapers, borders, bedding, needlework, and paper crafts. Donna has published nine books with North Light; her most recent is *Painting Fabulous Flowers with Donna Dewberry*.

A NOTE FROM DONNA

This year has been one of many reflections regarding my role as a mother. I remember the days when, as a young mother, I desired so much to have a proper flower garden. But with seven children and their assorted pets, it just wasn't possible. Every time I attempted to cultivate such a garden I usually found myself in utter frustration. I was either lacking the time such a garden required, or the wish for a garden was always outweighed by the childrens' needs for a soccer field or other comparable backyard sports complex. It seemed as though my wish would always be just that, a wish.

Now that all my children have grown and left the nest I am finally able to have that garden I always dreamed of. After much negotiation with my husband and lots of hard work (mostly on the part of others!), I finally realized my garden. I'm able to stroll among the assorted flowers and many exotic plants and enjoy their beauty. I do love looking out onto my garden but do you know what's funny? I think of my children and my grandchildren. I picture them running and playing in my garden and I'm not the least bit upset. I realize now more than ever that my role as a mother has been the one that allowed the most growth in my life, and even though a garden is wonderful, I would never trade motherhood for anything.

I acknowledge mothers everywhere and recognize their invaluable role in our world. No, I wasn't the perfect mother and being perfect probably isn't going to happen for very many of us, but the role I was blessed with as a mother is one that is priceless to me. My real garden has been my children and my dream was always there—it just took a little time to realize it.

A SPECIAL THANK YOU...

To the Newport Garden Club in Northern Kentucky, and the Cincinnati Civic Garden Center for so graciously allowing us to photograph in their beautiful surroundings and for their kind assistance with the preparations and planning.

I dedicate this book to my children and grandchildren. May they grow even more strong and beautiful each day. I am thankful for each of them. My garden is full and the dream has been realized. Thank you.

Love, Mom

Contents

1. Materials Needed 8
   Paints and Mediums
   Brushes
   Palettes
   Miscellaneous Supplies

2. How to Load the Brush 12
   Double loading
   Sideloading
   Sideload Float
   Multi-loading
   Loading a Script Liner
   Loading a Fan Brush
   Loading a Sponge Painter

3. Painting Leaves 16
   Simple one-stroke leaf
   Long, slender leaf
   Layered C-stroke leaf
   Wiggle-edge leaf
   Wiggle-edge with one smooth side
   Maple leaf
   Palm fronds
   Grasses

4. Painting Petals 20
   Easy daisy petals
   Chisel-edge petal strokes
   Tulip petals
   Seashell petal stroke
   Jagged-edge petal
   Layered five-petal flowers
   Pointed hydrangea petal
   Lily petal stroke
   Ruffled-edge petals
   Trailing flower petals

Welcome to My Garden!

37 easy-to-paint projects for your porch, patio, yard and garden 24

  1. *Garden Insect Stakes* 26

  2. *Four-Season Address Signs* 32

  3. *Butterfly Houses.* 42

  4. *Outdoor Beverage Cabinet* 50

  5. *At the Beach* 54

  6. *Magnolias Outdoor Clock* 60

  7. *For the Gardener* 66

  8. *Evening Lights* 72

  9. *Pillows for the Porch* 80

10. *Wildflower Planter.* 86

11. *Garden Tools Mailbox.* 90

12. *Windowbox with Daylilies* 94

13. *Terra Cotta Wall Planters* 98

14. *Berry Pretty Wind Chimes* 104

15. *Romantic Floral Swing* 110

Gallery of Garden Décor Ideas 116

Resources 118

Index. 118

Tear-out Color Recipe Cards. 121

Materials Needed

PAINTS AND MEDIUMS

ACRYLIC PAINTS

Plaid FolkArt acrylic colors are high-quality acrylic paints that come in handy 2-oz. (59ml) squeeze bottles. Their rich and creamy formulation and long open time make them perfect for decorative painting. They are offered in a wide range of wonderful pre-mixed colors.

ENAMELS

FolkArt Enamels are the ultimate one-step, dishwasher-safe paints for glass, ceramics, metal and other slick reflective surfaces. These revolutionary paints are highly pigmented and go on rich and creamy. There are a few general instructions for using Enamels paints:

- Always clean a glass surface with rubbing alcohol; you need to remove dirt and skin oils. Be careful not to touch the areas you are painting.
- Always follow the manufacturer's instructions for baking and washing the painted surface.
- Do not use in direct contact with food. And never cut on a surface that has been painted.
- Don't use water to thin Enamels; use Clear Medium to moisten the bristles and to thin the paint.

If you are painting a stroke of Enamels paint on top of an existing stroke, there are a couple of things that you need to keep in mind:

- If the paint of the first stroke is completely wet or completely dry, then painting a stroke on top will give you satisfactory results. If the paint is partially wet (such as having one edge that is thicker), then painting a stroke over that one edge will cause the wet parts of the first stroke to lift, resulting in unde-

sirable splotches of thin and thick paint. To avoid this problem, allow any strokes that will be overlapped to completely dry before painting over. Use a blow dryer to quicken the drying process if needed.
- All Enamels painting must be completed within 24 hours of starting a project. Any paint applied after 24 hours or after baking will not fuse properly and will not have the same dura- bility.

OUTDOOR PAINTS

FolkArt Outdoor Opaques and Dimensional paints can be used on a variety of surfaces: unpainted or painted metal, tin, terra cotta, wood, stone and concrete. Outdoor paint is made with a sealer in it. It has been lab tested to withstand normal weather conditions equivalent to 3-5 years. Do not mix water with this paint. Water will dilute the sealer and cause less durability. Instead, use Outdoor Flow Medium to moisten the brush or thin the paint.

For more protection from the weather and sun, use a spray lacquer finish (satin or gloss) on any painted item that will be used in your garden or on an open-air patio or deck.

MEDIUMS

FolkArt Floating Medium is a clear gel that is specially formulated for "floating" acrylic colors. It won't run like water can, and it dries quickly without extenders. I use it often to make my acrylic colors more transparent and to float shading around and between flower petals and leaves, and to add shadows.

FolkArt Outdoor Flow Medium thins Outdoor paints for shading and easy line work. Painted pieces will maintain their rich color, even when left out in the weather.

FolkArt Enamels Clear Medium is used with Enamels paints to achieve just the right paint consistency for effects such as shadows and shading without compromising the paint's adhesion or durability.

PAINTING SUPPLIES

PALETTE

The FolkArt One Stroke Paint Palette (top, facing page) is a circular palette with a number of paint wells for your colors and floating medium, holes for your brushes and a place for paper towels. I use 9-inch (23cm) disposable foam plates to put my paints on, and the tabs on the palette hold the plates in place. The palette is comfortable to hold and easy to clean.

DOUBLE-LOADING CAROUSEL

To make double-loading your brushes even easier, the One Stroke Double Loading Carousel (top, this page) allows you to pick up just the right amount of paint on your flat brushes. It has sixteen wedge-shaped wells for your colors, and a center well for floating medium. It comes with a sponge that can be dampened and a sealed lid to keep your acrylic paints fresh and moist longer. It even fits in the circular paint palette shown at top on the facing page.

BRUSH CADDY

The One Stroke Brush Caddy is one of my favorite multi-tasking tools for painting. It holds rinse water in two separate basins to clean paint out of your brushes, and it provides holes along the side to store your wet brushes in a safe manner that protects the bristles.

SPONGE PAINTERS AND STRETCHED CANVAS

FolkArt Sponge Painters come in two sizes and have a rounded end and a pointed end which allows you to sponge on faux finishes or basecoats in tight spaces and corners. Use the flat side to cover large areas. For the tropical beach scene on pages 54-59, I painted on stretched canvas with wide sides (shown below) onto which I continued the design on all four sides. No framing needed!

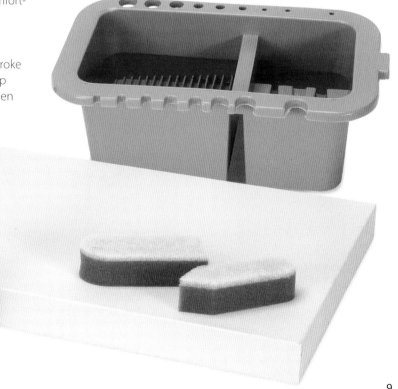

BRUSHES

FLATS

Painting the One-Stroke technique requires the use of flat brushes. Flats are designed with longer bristles and less thickness in the body of the bristles to allow for a much sharper chisel edge. In the instructions for the painting projects in this book, I often say "begin on the chisel edge" or "lift back up to the chisel edge." A sharp chisel edge is essential to the success of your painting as most of the strokes begin and end on the chisel edge.

FILBERT, ANGULAR, RAKE AND FAN BRUSHES

A filbert brush is a flat brush with a chisel edge that has been cut into a curve. This brush creates a rounder outer edge on the petals of flowers such as daisies and lilacs.

An angular, or angle, brush is also a flat brush with a chisel edge, but its bristles are trimmed at an angle, making one side longer (the toe) than the other side (heel). The angular brush makes painting comma strokes much easier.

The rake (or feather) brush is a flat brush whose bristles thin out along the chisel edge. I use this brush to paint feathery blossoms and palm fronds. A fan brush is great for painting grasses.

SCRUFFY BRUSHES

Scruffy brushes come in several sizes from very large to very small. I use them to pounce on flower centers, faux finishes and shading textures, among others. The scruffy brush is ready to be used straight out of the package. All you have to do is "fluff the scruff," as

3/4-INCH (19MM) FLAT

NO. 10 FILBERT

5/8-INCH (16MM) ANGULAR

1/2-INCH (13MM) RAKE

3/4-INCH (19MM) SCRUFFY BRUSH

NO. 8 ROUND

NO. 2 SCRIPT LINER

NO. 1 LINER

8/0 LINER

we say. Remove the brush from the packaging and form the natural hair bristles into an oval shape by gently pulling on them. Then twist the bristles in the palm of your hand until you have a nice oval shape. Now you are ready to pounce into paint and begin. Do not use water when painting with a scruffy brush.

When it's time to clean the scruffy brush, you'll need to pounce the bristles into the brush basin. Do not rake them across the ribbing in the bottom or you will break the natural hair bristles.

ROUNDS AND SCRIPT LINERS
A round brush can be used to paint scrolls, flower petals, leaves and lettering. It holds a lot of paint and the roundness eliminates sharp edges, making elegant strokes easy.

Script liners are round brushes with very thin bristles. Use these with "inky" paint for curlicues and tendrils, and with regular paint to dot in flower centers.

GLASS AND CERAMICS BRUSHES
Developed for use with FolkArt Enamels paints, these brushes feature softer bristles and allow for smooth paint application on non-porous surfaces such as glass, china, ceramics and metal.

BRUSHES FOR PAPER
Stiffer bristles make these brushes ideal for painting on paper, but they are also ideal for painting on fabrics. I used these brushes to paint on the fabric porch pillows shown on pages 80-83.

NO. 4 FAN BRUSH

1/2-INCH (13MM) MOP BRUSH

NO. 12 FLAT BRUSH FOR GLASS & CERAMICS

3/8-INCH (10MM) ANGULAR FOR GLASS & CERAMICS

1/8-INCH (3MM) SCRUFFY FOR GLASS & CERAMICS

NO. 2 SCRIPT LINER FOR GLASS & CERAMICS

NO. 12 FLAT BRUSH FOR PAPER

NO. 2 SCRIPT LINER FOR PAPER

How to Load the Brush

chisel edge

flat side   ferrule   handle   tip end of handle

DOUBLE-LOADING A FLAT BRUSH

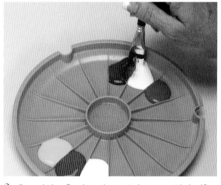

1. Using the Double Loading Carousel, place puddles of paint in the wedge-shaped sections of the carousel. Place the colors you'll be double loading next to each other. Here, on the left side of the carousel, I've placed Pure Orange in the middle, Yellow Light on one side and Wicker White on the other. Another option on the right side of the carousel is Wicker White in the middle, Magenta on one side, and Periwinkle on the other. The idea is to put the color you would use most in the middle so you can double load from either side.

2. Stand the flat brush straight up with half the bristles in one color and half in the other. Stroke back and forth to fill the bristles with paint. The carousel's divided wedges keep the colors separate for you.

3. Move your brush to an open wedge and work the paint into the bristles. If you don't have any open wedges available, use your palette or a foam plate for this. Keep your loading spot no more than 1-1/2 inches (38mm) to 2 inches (51mm) long. Don't allow it to stretch longer and longer as you work the paint into the bristles.

4. This is a correctly loaded flat brush. Your bristles should be no more than two-thirds full with paint.

5. This is what a good double-loaded stroke looks like. The colors blend smoothly in the middle with no sharp dividing line.

DOUBLE-LOADING AN ANGULAR BRUSH

Heel. On an angular brush, the heel is the shorter side of the bristles.

Toe. The toe is the longer side of the bristles. Hold the brush so the toe is at the top.

1. Dampen the brush. Stroke between the two puddles of color. Here, I'm loading Magenta onto the heel and Wicker White onto the toe.

2. Work the colors into the bristles. Pick up more paint as you stroke. It takes quite a few strokes to get the toe fully loaded with color.

3. This is how a properly loaded angular brush should look.

SIDELOADING A FLAT BRUSH

1. To sideload your brush, begin by working some floating medium into the bristles of a flat brush.

2. Stroke through the edge of the puddle of paint to pick up a little color on the edge of the brush. Work this into your bristles by stroking back and forth.

SIDELOAD FLOAT

This is what a successful sideload float looks like. Use sideload floats to shade around the outer edge of any object to make it stand out from the background, or between objects such as leaves and flowers where there would naturally be a shadow.

DOUBLE-LOADING A FILBERT BRUSH

1. Dampen your filbert brush with water. Pull paint outward from the edge of your first puddle of color.

2. Flip the brush over to the other side. Pull the second color out from the edge of the puddle.

3. When you stroke with the loaded filbert, the key thing to remember is that the color facing upward is the dominant color. Here it's the orange.

4. But here the dominant color is the yellow because the yellow side of the brush is facing upward.

DOUBLE-LOADING A SCRUFFY BRUSH

1. A scruffy brush is loaded differently than a flat. Never dampen it first with water, and never dip it into the middle of a paint puddle. Instead, pounce the scruffy at the edge of the puddle to load half of the brush with the first color.

2. This shows how only half of the bristles are loaded with paint so far.

3. Now pounce the other side of the scruffy into the edge of the puddle of the second color.

4. Now you can see how the brush is evenly double-loaded with the two colors.

MULTI-LOADING A FLAT BRUSH

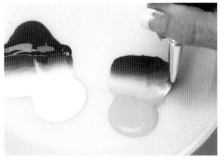

1. Double load a flat brush with your first two colors. Work the paint into the bristles by stroking back and forth in the loading zone. Here I'm loading Magenta and Wicker White.

2. Sideload the brush into your third color. This is Yellow Light.

3. Here you can clearly see all three colors. A multi-loaded brush makes a great flower petal in just one stroke.

MULTI-LOADING A FAN BRUSH

1. I often use a fan brush to paint grasses quickly and easily. Start with a dry brush and tap the bristles into the first color. This is Thicket.

2. Tap one side of the brush into the edge of the puddle of the second color. This is Fresh Foliage.

3. Tap the same side of the brush into the edge of the puddle of a third color, Yellow Light.

4. Tap your multi-loaded fan brush onto the palette to remove excess paint. Here you can see all three colors.

LOADING A SCRIPT LINER WITH INKY PAINT

1. Place a few droplets of clean water on your palette next to the puddle of paint, using a no. 2 script liner.

2. Pull a little paint into the water droplets making a circular motion with your brush.

3. Dip your brush into clean water three times as you continue to pull paint out into the inky puddle.

4. As you pull the brush out of the puddle, roll the brush in your fingers and drag the tip of the bristles on the palette to bring them to a point.

DOUBLE-LOADING A SPONGE PAINTER

1. I use a sponge painter when I need to cover a large area, such as the sky and water in the painting on page 54. Dampen the sponge and pick up some floating medium. Pull out some Wicker White on the top edge of the sponge.

2. Then pull out some Cobalt Blue from the edge of the puddle. This is how your double-loaded sponge should look.

3. Use lateral strokes to paint the sky or water. The colors will vary, giving a more natural look. Pick up more floating medium when you need to reload your two colors.

Painting Leaves

SIMPLE ONE-STROKE LEAF

1. Double load a flat brush with a lighter green and a darker green. Begin on the chisel edge and then push down to fan out the bristles.

2. Lift back up to the chisel edge to finish the stroke.

3. Pull a stem partway into the leaf, using the chisel edge of the brush.

LONG, SLENDER LEAF

  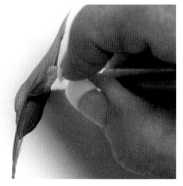

1. Double load a flat brush with a lighter green and a darker green. Start on the chisel edge at an angle and begin sliding upward from the base.

2. Continue sliding to the tip and lift back up to the chisel edge to form a point. Make sure you don't turn your brush. It should still be at the same angle at which you started.

3. Pull a stem partway into the leaf, using the chisel edge of the brush.

LAYERED C-STROKE LEAF

1. Double load a flat brush with a lighter green and a darker green. Start at the base of the leaf with an open C-stroke.

2. Paint another open C-stroke overlapping the first one.

3. Continue to layer more open C-strokes that get smaller and smaller as you get closer to the tip of the leaf. They also get less curvy.

4. Repeat for the other half of the leaf. For the final C-stroke, lift to the chisel to form a sharp point at the tip of the leaf. Pull a stem partway into the base of the leaf.

WIGGLE-EDGE LEAF

1. Double load a flat brush with a lighter green and a darker green. Touch the chisel edge of the brush to the surface to make two V-shaped guidelines for the base of the leaf. Start at one guideline, press down on the bristles and wiggle the brush to make a seashell stroke.

2. Continue to wiggle up to the tip, lifting to the chisel to form a point. The closer you get to the tip, the smaller your wiggle motion should be.

3. For the other half of the leaf, start at the other guideline (see Step 1 photo) and wiggle up to the tip, lifting to the chisel to form a point.

4. Pull a stem partway into the base of the leaf.

WIGGLE-EDGE LEAF WITH ONE SMOOTH SIDE

1. Double load a flat brush. Follow Steps 1 and 2 above to form the wiggle-edge half of the leaf. For the smooth side, start at the base, press down and slide smoothly upward.

2. Lift back up to the chisel as you slide to the tip of the leaf, leading with the lighter green side of the brush.

3. Pull a stem partway into the leaf to finish.

1. To begin, double load a flat brush with Pure Orange and Soft Apple. Pick up some Yellow Light on the green side. Start at the base of the leaf, push down on the bristles and wiggle up to a point. Slide smoothly back down to the base. This is the first lobe of the maple leaf.

2. The second lobe of the leaf is smaller and partially overlaps the first. Wiggle a couple of times up to the point and slide smoothly back to the base of the second lobe.

3. For the third and final lobe, wiggle out and lift to the chisel as you slide to the tip. Do not slide back down to the base.

4. Reload your brush and begin the second half of the leaf at the base again. Paint the first lobe the same as you did in Step 1, flipping the brush to keep the orange to the outside.

5. Paint the second lobe same as you did in Step 2. Remember, this lobe is smaller and overlaps the first one.

6. Wiggle out to the tip, lifting back up to the chisel edge to form a point.

7. Pull a stem partway into the leaf, leading with the green side of your brush.

PALM FRONDS

1. Painting palm trees with a rake or feather brush is easy and fun! Begin by placing the center stem of the palm frond with the chisel edge of a flat brush. Pick up inky Thicket on the flat side of the rake brush, then pick up Aqua on the same side. Pull fronds from the stem outward, starting at the base of the stem. Flick the brush upward as you get to the tips of the fronds to create sharp points.

2. Pull fronds on the other side of the center stem, starting at the base again. These fronds are shorter to show that the palm leaves are turned.

3. With the chisel edge of the flat brush, pull a stem up the center again to clean up and re-establish the stem.

GRASSES

1. Multi-load a no. 4 fan brush with Thicket, Fresh Foliage and Yellow Light, following the instructions on page 15. Tap the fan brush lightly on the surface to create little hills and fields of grass. Using a fan brush means you do not have to paint every individual blade of grass. The splayed-out bristles of the fan make quick work of it.

2. Add a little water to your dark green to make it inky and load your fan brush on one side. Don't rinse or clean your brush first.

3. To create tall grasses and foliage, stroke upward with the fine hairs along the outside edge of the fan brush. Apply almost no pressure to keep these grasses light and airy.

4. To create finer, shorter grasses along the tops of the hills, use the rake brush and inky green paint. It's easier to control the shape of these grasses with the rake rather than the fan brush.

Painting Petals

EASY DAISY PETALS

1. Double load a flat brush with Periwinkle and Wicker White. Begin at the outer end of the first petal and push down hard as you start to pull the stroke toward you.

2. Slide to the base of the petal as you lift back up to the chisel edge to finish the stroke.

3. To form a daisy blossom, it's easiest to think of it as a clock face. Place four strokes in the 12, 3, 6 and 9 o'clock positions to start.

4. Then add a petal stroke in between those four strokes. Continue filling in with daisy petal strokes. Turn your surface as you go to make painting easier.

5. Don't try to make each petal exactly the same. It looks more natural if some are slightly wider or longer than others. Just make sure you pull all the strokes to the same center point.

CHISEL-EDGE PETAL STROKES

1. Double load a flat brush with Periwinkle and Wicker White. Pull a single stroke, staying up on the chisel edge of the brush.

2. Add more chisel-edge strokes on both sides, all ending in a point at the base. This is the back layer of petals.

3. Now flip your brush so the Wicker White is on the other side and stroke a second layer of petals. Bring these to a point at the base.

4. Flip your brush again so the Periwinkle is on the other side, and stroke another layer of petals, again bringing them to a point at the base. Fan these out to the sides and make a few shorter.

WIGGLE-EDGE TULIP PETAL

1. Double load a flat brush with Magenta and Yellow Light plus floating medium. Begin at the base and wiggle up to the tip.

2. Without turning or pivoting your brush, wiggle back down to the base of the petal.

TULIP PETAL WITH ONE SMOOTH SIDE

1. Double load a flat brush with Magenta and Yellow Light plus floating medium. Begin at the base and wiggle up to the tip.

2. Without turning or pivoting your brush, slide smoothly back down to the base.

SEASHELL PETAL STROKE

1. Multi-load a flat brush with Magenta on one side and Yellow Light and Wicker White on the other. Start at the base, wiggle out and slide back half way. Repeat for each ruffled segment.

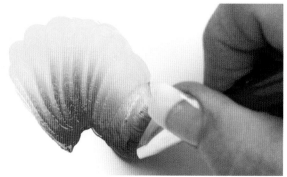

2. Continue to wiggle out and slide back until your petal is the size you need. Finish by sliding back all the way to the base and lifting to the chisel.

JAGGED-EDGE PETAL

1. Double load a no. 12 flat brush with Magenta and Wicker White. Start on the chisel edge, touch, and lean toward the flat side of the brush. Use quick zig-zag motions to create the jagged edge.

2. When your petal is the size you need, lift back up to the chisel and slide to the base.

LAYERED FIVE-PETAL FLOWERS

1. Each petal of a five-petal flower is a teardrop petal stroke. Double load a no. 12 flat with Cobalt Blue and Wicker White. Begin the teardrop shape by touching the chisel to the surface and pushing down, which flares the bristles out. Stroke up and over without turning or pivoting your brush.

2. Continue the stroke, lifting to the chisel and ending at the pointed base of the petal.

3. A five-petal flower is a series of teardrop petal strokes all started from the same center point. To layer your five-petal flowers, start with a cluster of three teardrop petals. Keep the blue side of the brush to the outside edge of each petal.

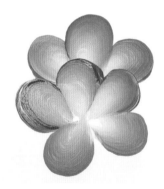

4. Layer another cluster of three teardrop petals in front.

5. Complete this cluster by adding two more petals below the three you painted in Step 4.

6. For color variations, flip the brush so the Wicker White side is to the outside edge of the petals, and paint a five-petal cluster. Finish by dotting the centers with Yellow Light. Paint large hydrangea blossoms by grouping lots of five-petal flowers together in a rounded cluster.

POINTED HYDRANGEA PETAL

1. Many hydrangea petals have little points on the ends. Double load a flat brush with your petal colors. Start at the base, push down to form the widest part, then lift to the chisel at the tip but don't lift your brush off the surface.

2. Begin sliding back down to form the little point, then push down on the bristles to widen the petal, and finish at the base.

LILY PETAL STROKE

1. Double load a no. 12 flat with orange and yellow and dip into floating medium. Begin on the chisel, push down as you slide up to widen the middle, then stand back up to the chisel to make a sharp point at the tip but do not lift your brush off the surface.

2. Slide back down from the tip, pushing down on the bristles to widen the middle.

3. As you lift back up to the chisel, slightly turn the brush toward the middle of the petal to curl the edge, then slide on the chisel to the base.

RUFFLED-EDGE PETALS

1. Double load a flat with Yellow Ochre and Wicker White. Start on the chisel and wiggle out a few times to paint a single petal.

2. Slide back to the pointed base and lift back up to the chisel.

3. Paint a series of ruffled-edge petals all radiating outward from a center point. Turn your surface to make painting easier.

4. Dot the center with Fresh Foliage on the tip end of the brush handle.

TRAILING FLOWER PETALS

1. For trailing flowers or buds, always start at the bottom or outermost tip and work your way to the top. Double load a small flat brush with Magenta and Yellow Light. Touch down on the chisel and pull upward to make a very short stroke.

2. The middle of the cluster is tight little C-strokes that partially overlap the lower strokes. Widen and fan out as you work upwards.

3. At the top of the cluster, use more open C-strokes to paint larger petals or buds, partially overlapping the smaller ones below.

Welcome to my garden!

I love painting things for my garden, especially now that we have wonderful paints that are durable in the weather and don't fade in the sun! Plus, there are now lots of decorative yard and garden accessories available that will dress up anyone's outdoor areas. These are easy to find at garden stores and craft stores.

Nowadays, almost any decorative item you have indoors is also made for the outdoors. The projects on the following pages make good use of these new decorative items. They're fun to paint and they'll add a personal touch to all your outdoor spaces, whether it's a small front porch, a back deck, a patio, or a place where the family grills out and enjoys warm summer evenings.

Now, gather up your paints and let's take a walk through the garden.

Garden Insect Stakes

Brushes
3/4-inch (19mm) flat
1-inch (25mm) flat
nos. 10 and 12 flats
nos. 1 and 2 script liners

Surfaces
Wooden cutouts made
on a bandsaw

Additional Supplies
FolkArt Flow Medium
Metal stakes

Bring fun and whimsy to your garden with cute and colorful insect stakes! All your favorite bugs are here: a bright red ladybug, a couple of fluttering butterflies and some pretty blue dragonflies. Each one was painted on lightweight wooden cutouts with durable Outdoor paints that withstand weather and garden hoses. I attached mine to long metal stakes and sank them deeply into my garden beds to keep them stable in the wind. These are fun and easy projects you can do with your kids. Let them choose their favorite colors for their bugs as I did for mine. Blue butterflies? Why not?

FOLKART OUTDOOR METALLICS

Metallic Blue Sapphire   Metallic Emerald Green

FOLKART OUTDOOR OPAQUES

Engine Red   Berry Wine   Licorice   Wicker White

Cobalt   School Bus Yellow   Lemon Custard

Ladybug

1. Wings. Basecoat the wooden cutout with Wicker White and let dry. Load a 3/4-inch (19mm) flat with Engine Red and sideload into Berry Wine. Paint the red wings. Keep the Berry Wine to the outside to shade and shape the wings along the outside edge and down the center.

2. Body. Base the body and head with Licorice on a 3/4-inch (19mm) flat. Sideload the dirty brush into Wicker White to separate and highlight the head.

3. Antennae and Wing Spots. Detail the antennae with Licorice on a no. 1 script liner. Double load a no. 10 flat with Wicker White and Licorice and paint the spots on the wings in two half-circle strokes, keeping the Wicker White to the outside.

4. Final Details. The swirls on the spots are added with Wicker White on a no. 1 script liner. Outline the wings with Licorice on a no. 1 script liner.

Blue Butterfly

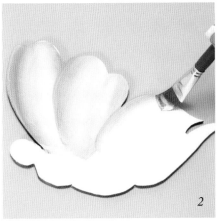

1

2

3

1. Load the Brush. Basecoat the wooden cutout with Wicker White and let dry. Begin by double-loading Metallic Blue Sapphire and Wicker White on a 1-inch (25mm) flat. Dip into Floating Medium and work out some of the paint on your palette first so it becomes very transparent.

2. Wings. Paint the wing segments with long, smooth strokes starting at the body and working outward.

3. Body. The body is Cobalt with Wicker White plus a tiny bit of Licorice on a 1-inch (25mm) flat. Paint large C-strokes or curves for the segments. The lower body is Cobalt without any Licorice or Wicker White.

4. Wings. Define and separate the wing segments with Licorice on a no. 10 flat.

5. Final Details. Use a no. 10 flat to paint circles and comma strokes on the wings with School Bus Yellow + Wicker White. Use Wicker White to place comma strokes on the body. Load a no. 2 script liner with inky Licorice to paint the face, antennae, fine lines on the wings, and shading on the commas and spots.

4

Orange and Yellow Butterfly

1

2

3

1. Wings. Basecoat the wooden cutout with Wicker White and let dry. Load Lemon Custard on a 1-inch (25mm) flat and pick up Floating Medium. Basecoat the lower wings. Sideload the same brush into Engine Red and shade the outer edges of the wings.

2. Outline. Load a no. 12 flat with Licorice and outline the wing shapes to separate the upper and lower wings.

3. Body. With the same brush and Licorice, paint the vein lines on the wings using the chisel edge of the brush. Base in the body with Licorice.

4. Final Details. The spots on the wings are Licorice and Wicker White for the big ones. Use the handle end of the brush for the small dots. Paint Wicker White accents on the wings, and curving lines to segment the body.

Blue Dragonflies

1. *Wings*. Basecoat the wooden cutout with Wicker White and let dry. Paint the wing segments with a 1-inch (25mm) flat and Wicker White + Metallic Emerald Green + lots of Floating Medium—mostly Wicker White so there's just a hint of color. Pick up Metallic Blue Sapphire occasionally.

2. *Body*. Load Metallic Blue Sapphire + Wicker White on one side of the brush. Sideload into Metallic Emerald Green and paint large C-strokes for the body segments. Allow the Metallic Emerald Green to create the body segments. On the lower body, flip the brush so the Wicker White side of the brush creates the segments.

3. *Outline*. Load a no. 2 script liner with inky Licorice and outline the wings. Add very fine vein lines of inky Licorice.

4. *Final Details*. Detail the face, body and antennae with the same brush and inky Licorice.

5. *Full Dragonfly*. Basecoat the wooden cutout with Wicker White and let dry. Paint this dragonfly with the same brush and colors used in Steps 1 through 4.

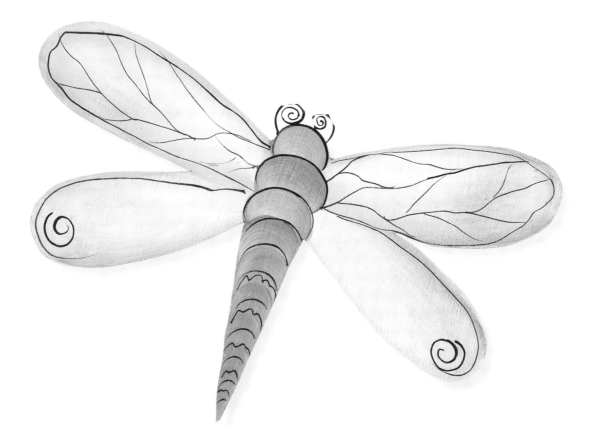

Four-Season Address Signs

Brushes
3⁄4-inch (19mm) flat
nos. 2, 6, 8, 12 and 16 flats
1⁄2-inch (13mm) scruffy
1⁄2-inch (13mm) mop
nos. 1 and 2 script liners

Surfaces
Arched-top wooden plaques
from Walnut Hollow

Additional Supplies
FolkArt Sponge Painters
FolkArt Flow Medium

*W*elcome guests to your home with a bright and colorful address sign you have painted yourself. There's a new one for each season in this project! When spring rolls around, you can paint these pretty spring flowers in soft pastels to echo the daffodils and tulips in your front yard. This wooden plaque can be hung on your front door, your porch wall, or displayed in your front yard. They're painted with durable Outdoor paints to hold up to all kinds of weather. For even more protection, give them a couple coats of spray lacquer in a satin or gloss finish.

FOLKART OUTDOOR DIMENSIONALS

Fresh Foliage   Wicker White   Lemon Custard

FOLKART OUTDOOR OPAQUES

Fresh Foliage   Yellow Ochre   Wicker White   School Bus Yellow   Magenta

Purple Lilac   Thicket   Light Blue   Pure Orange   Engine Red

Berry Wine   Burnt Umber   Cobalt

1. *Background.* Basecoat sign with Wicker White Outdoor paint. Let dry. Dampen sponge painter, load Fresh Foliage Outdoor Opaque and Flow Medium, and sponge on the background.

2. *Address Numbers.* Paint your address numbers with Fresh Foliage on a no. 8 flat. Freehand them or trace from a stencil.

3. *Yellow Rose.* The yellow rose at the top is Yellow Ochre loaded on a 3⁄4-inch (19mm) flat, sideloaded into Wicker White.

4. *Yellow Tulip.* The large yellow tulip in the center and the hanging bud is Yellow Ochre + Wicker White on a 3⁄4-inch (19mm) flat. Pick up a little School Bus Yellow on the Yellow Ochre side.

5. *Pink Flower.* On the dirty brush, pick up a little Magenta and paint the pink flower with teardrop petals.

6. *Lavender Roses.* Double load Purple Lilac and Wicker White on the 3⁄4-inch (19mm) flat and paint the lavender roses.

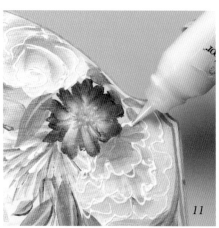

7. *Lavender Daisy*. Pick up a little bit of Magenta on the dirty brush (Purple Lilac + Wicker White) and paint the large lavender daisy at the top. Pick up a little more Magenta for the daisy buds at the sides of the board. The large yellow daisy at top is School Bus Yellow + Wicker White.

8. *Yellow-pink Tulip*. The yellow-pink tulip is Magenta + School Bus Yellow on a 3⁄4-inch (19mm) flat, plus a little Wicker White. Double load Magenta + Wicker White on a no. 12 flat and paint the jagged-edge petals of the dark pink flowers (see finished address board below right).

9. *Flower Centers*. Add the centers on the large daisies with the 1⁄2-inch (13mm) scruffy loaded with School Bus Yellow and Fresh Foliage. Highlight with Wicker White. Use dimensional Fresh Foliage and Wicker White to dot on the anthers. The leaves are Fresh Foliage on a no. 12 or no. 6 flat depending on size.

10. *Shading*. Use inky Thicket on a no. 2 script liner to shade the address numbers. Outline the plaque with inky Fresh Foliage on a script liner.

11. *Outline Petals*. Outline the petals on some flowers with Wicker White Outdoor Dimensional paint.

Summer

1. Background. Basecoat the sign with Wicker White. Let dry. With a dampened sponge, streak lateral strokes of Light Blue thinned with Flow Medium for a blue-sky look.

2. Tiger Lily. Pencil in where you want your design to go, referring to the finished sign on the next page. Double load School Bus Yellow and Pure Orange, then sideload into Engine Red. Paint the back petals of the tiger lily. Start at the base of each petal, slide smoothly to the tip, then slide smoothly back to the base.

3. Tiger Lily. Add the backsides of the front petals that extend down from the top.

4. Veins. With Fresh Foliage on a 3/4-inch (19mm) flat, chisel edge the center veins on the petals.

5. Stem and Leaves. Pick up Thicket on your dirty brush and add a stem for the lower tiger lily and paint the large leaves.

6. Outlining. Load inky Engine Red on a no. 2 script liner and outline the lily petals, ending with a little curve on the tip to add graceful form to the petals. Using the same brush, outline the edge of the plaque following the shape by bracing your little finger against the edge.

7. *Address Numbers.* Load a no. 8 flat with Fresh Foliage and paint your address numbers.

8. *Shading.* Load a no. 1 script liner with Thicket and add a shaded edge to each number, embellishing the shading lines with extra loops and curves if you wish.

9. *Petal Details.* Dab specks randomly on the insides of the lily petals with Berry Wine on a no. 2 flat.

10. *Anthers.* To add the anthers, use Fresh Foliage Outdoor Dimensional. Start at the outside tip and pull upward toward the flower centers. Add yellow pollen dots with Lemon Custard Outdoor Dimensional.

Autumn

1. *Background.* Basecoat the sign with Wicker White. Let dry. Dampen a sponge painter, then pick up some Burnt Umber thinned with Flow Medium and paint the background with lateral strokes. Concentrate this color mostly around the edges, letting it fade off into the center.

2. *Address Numbers.* Paint your address numbers with Burnt Umber on a no. 8 flat. Freehand them or use a number stencil.

3. *Branches.* Place the branches around the plaque with Burnt Umber and Wicker White double loaded on a no. 12 flat.

4. *Large Autumn Leaves.* Double load a 3⁄4-inch (19mm) flat with School Bus Yellow and Pure Orange. Paint the large leaves, keeping the orange to the outside. Pick up Burnt Umber on the chisel edge of the brush and pull stems into the leaves.

5. *Small Autumn Leaves.* Double load a no. 16 flat with School Bus Yellow and Pure Orange, then pick up a little Engine Red on the orange side. Paint the four smaller autumn leaves, varying the colors by flipping the brush over so the Engine Red is on the outside for one or two of the leaves. Pick up Fresh Foliage or Thicket on your brush to introduce some green into a few of the leaves.

6

7

8

9

6. *Acorns*. Add a branch for the acorns at the top that runs over the top leaf, using Burnt Umber + Wicker White. With the same dirty brush, pick up School Bus Yellow and a little Pure Orange and work the colors into the brush. Then paint heart shapes that come to a point to create the acorns.

7. *Acorn Caps*. Paint the acorn caps with the chisel edge of the brush and Burnt Umber.

8. *Filler Leaves*. Load a no. 12 flat with Engine Red and Burnt Umber and paint one or two clusters of long, slender, dark red leaves. Fill in the edges of the sign with different shapes and sizes of green leaves using Thicket and Fresh Foliage.

9. *Shading*. Load inky Burnt Umber onto a no. 2 script liner and paint the decorative border around the outside of the plaque. Load a no. 12 flat with Flow Medium, sideload into Burnt Umber and shade around the leaves and within the numbers.

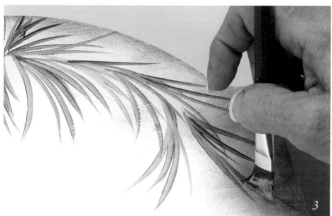

1. *Background.* Basecoat your sign with Wicker White and let dry. Dampen a sponge painter with water, dip the sponge edge into Flow Medium, then dip into a little Thicket. Sponge on the background color. Concentrate on the outside edges, fading into white in the center.

2. *Address Numbers.* Paint your address numbers using a no. 8 flat loaded with Thicket + Flow Medium.

3. *Pine Needles.* Stroke the long pine needles with Thicket and Fresh Foliage double loaded on a no. 16 flat. Stay up on the chisel edge and lead with the lighter green. Refer to the finished sign at right on the facing page for placement of the pine needles.

4. *Pine Cones.* Work Cobalt and Thicket into your no. 12 flat and pick up a little Wicker White on the blue side of the brush. Chisel-stroke the first layer of the pine cones, starting with the outer tip and pulling your strokes upward toward the stem where the cone attaches to the branch.

5. *Pine Cone Segments.* Reload your brush with Cobalt, Thicket and Wicker White and continue layering on the individual segments, overlapping them as you work upwards. Stroke randomly so the segments are not lined up—this gives a more natural look.

6

7

6. *Snow Detail.* With a 1/2-inch (13mm) mop brush, lightly dab Wicker White on the pine cones and some of the needles to create a light dusting of snow here and there.

7. *Shading.* Load a no. 2 script liner with inky Cobalt and shade the address numbers, then paint a thin borderline around the rim of the plaque. Highlight parts of the numbers with Wicker White on the no. 2 script liner.

Butterfly Houses

Brushes
nos. 8, 12 and 16 flats

Surface
Wooden butterfly houses
available at garden and
craft stores.

Additional Supplies
FolkArt Sponge Painters
FolkArt Flow Medium

*W*ouldn't you love to have all kinds of beautiful butterflies flitting around in your garden? Placing wooden houses made especially for butterflies will help attract them to your area. Butterfly houses are different from bird houses—the openings for butterflies must be very narrow vertical slits. They fold up their wings to get inside, and the small openings protect them from predators. These wooden houses were handmade for me by a dear friend, but you can easily buy similar ones at garden and craft stores during the spring and summer months. In this project we'll paint three different designs on three different size houses. Place them around your garden near a shallow water source and you'll attract many colorful "flutterbys."

FOLKART OUTDOOR DIMENSIONALS

Fresh Foliage	Wicker White	Lemon Custard

FOLKART OUTDOOR OPAQUES

Light Blue	Lemon Custard	Fresh Foliage	School Bus Yellow
Violet Pansy	Purple Lilac	Wicker White	Thicket
Pure Orange	Cobalt	Magenta	

Pansies with Yellow Butterflies

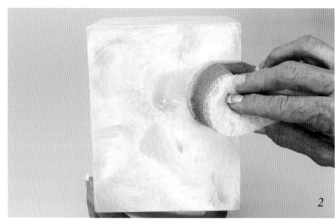

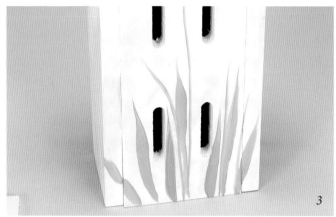

1. Background. Basecoat the medium size butterfly house with Wicker White and let dry. Using a sponge painter, sponge on Light Blue thinned with Flow Medium, fading out towards the top on the front and both sides.

2. Roof. On the roof, sponge on Lemon Custard and Fresh Foliage double loaded on a sponge painter.

3. Leaves and Stems. Double load a no. 12 flat with Fresh Foliage and School Bus Yellow and paint the long upright leaves and stems.

4. Purple Flowers. Double load Violet Pansy and Wicker White and paint the petals of the stalk flower with a push-down-and-pull motion.

5. Lower Petals. For the lower petals, touch the brush down at the outer tip of each petal and pull upward.

6. Centers. Dot in the purple flower centers with Lemon Custard Outdoor Dimensional paint.

7. Yellow Pansies. Paint the back petals of the yellow pansies with School Bus Yellow (occasionally lightened with Lemon Custard) double loaded with Wicker White on a no. 12 flat. Keep the white to the outside edges on all the petals.

8. Lower Petals. Paint the lower petals of the front pansies with the same brush and colors.

9. Purple Pansy. Double load a no. 12 flat with Violet Pansy and Wicker White. Touch into Lemon Custard with the white edge of the brush. Paint the purple pansy petals with seashell strokes.

10. Top Front Petal. Add the top front petal to the purple pansy, overlapping the two side petals.

11. Hairline Details. Use the chisel edge of the no. 8 flat and Violet Pansy to paint hairlines on the backs of the petals of the yellow pansies.

12. *Outline.* Dot Lemon Custard and Fresh Foliage Outdoor Dimensional paint in the pansy centers. Outline the petals with Wicker White Outdoor Dimensional using the tip of the bottle to draw on loose and wavy lines.

13. *Butterflies.* Paint the butterflies' wings with the same colors as the pansy petals. Zigzag the bodies and draw antennae with Fresh Foliage Dimensional paint. Detail the wings with Wicker White Dimensional.

Ask Donna

Q: If I can't find the exact same surfaces you painted on for these projects, what are some alternatives I can use instead?

A: Look for a shape that mimics the shape of the surface I painted on. Most of these designs can be altered to fit any shape, but laying out designs is the hardest part about painting. So if you are a beginner, choose a similar shape. For example, if you cannot find any butterfly houses, look for bird houses instead that have the same general shape. If you can't find the round clock shown on pages 60-65, paint on a charger plate or a round wooden plaque. Instead of the metal wind chimes shown on pages 104-109, make your own chimes by tying small terra cotta pots along a sturdy string. Paint the pots first before assembly. Don't have a bandsaw to cut out the garden bugs on pages 26-31? Paint the bug shape on a piece of square or round wood that has been basecoated green. At a distance the green will merge into the plants in your garden and the colorful bug will stand out.

Orange Daylilies and Blue Flowers

1. Leaves and Daylilies. Basecoat the small house with Wicker White and let dry. Using a sponge painter, sponge Light Blue on the house. Double load the sponge with Fresh Foliage and Lemon Custard and paint the roof. Paint the leaves and stems with Fresh Foliage and Thicket on a no. 12 flat. Double load Pure Orange and Lemon Custard on a no. 12 flat and paint the back petals of the daylilies and the two buds.

2. Front Petals. With the same colors and brush, add the front petals. Attach stems to the daylily blossoms with Thicket and Fresh Foliage.

3. Leaves. Paint large wiggle-edge leaves with Thicket and Fresh Foliage double loaded on a no. 12 flat.

4. Blue Flowers. Double load Cobalt and Wicker White on a no. 12 flat and paint the back layers of the blue five-petal flowers and the taller stalk flowers.

5. Flower Centers. Paint the front layers of petals with the same brush, flipped so the Wicker White is to the outside edge. Dot on the centers with Lemon Custard Dimensional paint.

6. Final Details. Paint the daylily anthers with Fresh Foliage Dimensional and add pollen dots with Lemon Custard Dimensional. Paint the butterfly wings with Lemon Custard and Wicker White. Make the body and antennae with Fresh Foliage Dimensional paint.

Pink Roses and Purple Flowers

1

2

3

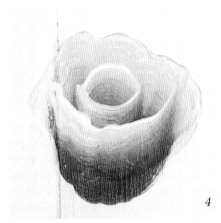

4

5

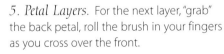

6

7

1. Stems and Leaves. Basecoat the tall butterfly house with Wicker White and let dry. Sponge Light Blue on the house and Fresh Foliage and Lemon Custard on the roof. Paint the vertical stems and the rose leaves with Fresh Foliage and Thicket, adding a little Wicker White. Pick up a little Magenta and tint some of the rose leaves.

2. Roses. Double load a no. 16 flat with Magenta and Wicker White and begin with the back petal of the open roses. Keep the Wicker White to the outside for all your rose petals.

3. Rose Center. Paint the center buds in the open roses with a U-stroke and a C-stroke.

4. Front Petal. The front petal of the open rose is shaped like a boat. Sweep the flat brush across the front of the center bud, starting on the chisel at the left side and ending on the chisel on the right side.

5. Petal Layers. For the next layer, "grab" the back petal, roll the brush in your fingers as you cross over the front.

6. Side Petals. Fit the side petals in underneath, pulling toward the center and lifting to the chisel.

7. Hanging Petals. The hanging petals have slightly ruffled edges. Keep the Wicker White to the outside edge.

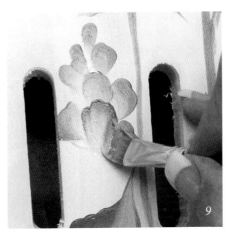

8. *Final Rose Petals.* Chisel-edge some more petals coming in from each side until you have enough layers.

9. *Purple Flowers.* Double load Purple Lilac and Wicker White and paint the lavender petals with a teardrop stroke that is slightly wiggled.

10. *Purple Flowers.* Flip the brush over so the Wicker White is more predominant and paint more petals.

11. *Butterflies.* Double load Violet Pansy and Wicker White and paint the open wings using ruffled-edge strokes.

12. *Butterflies.* Detail the wings with comma strokes of Lemon Custard and Wicker White. Paint the bodies and antennae with Fresh Foliage Dimensional paint.

Outdoor Beverage Cabinet

Brushes
1-inch (25mm) flat

Surface
Ready-to-assemble white cabinet from Target

Additional Supplies
Spray lacquer (optional)

*T*o keep your beverages, glasses and ice buckets clean and neatly stored for your next picnic on the patio, a two-door cabinet like this one serves many purposes. You can keep a set of drink glasses in the bottom drawer and bottles of soda and water on the inside shelves. When it's time for a party, set everything out on the top and let guests help themselves. I've painted this cabinet with banana leaves and palm fronds for a warm and welcoming tropical look. The cabinet's smooth white finish makes painting a breeze. When the paint is dry, I suggest using an exterior grade spray lacquer in a satin or glossy finish (whichever matches the finish on your cabinet) to protect the painting and keep it looking fresh and clean for years to come.

FOLKART OUTDOOR OPAQUES

Butter Pecan   Wicker White

FOLKART OUTDOOR METALLICS

Inca Gold
Metallic

Banana Leaves

1. Begin the Design. This design begins in the lower left and crosses over the cabinet doors. If it makes painting easier for you, remove the knobs first. Always start your design by placing the main stems.

2. Banana Leaf. Double load a 1-inch (25mm) flat with Butter Pecan and Inca Gold Metallic. Pick up a little Wicker White on the Gold side. Outline the outside shape of the banana leaf using the chisel edge, then use the flat side to pull inward toward the stem.

3. Lower Leaf. To paint the lower part of the banana leaf, start at the stem and pull downward. Keep reloading your brush with paint—it's the color variations in your brush that create the leaf segments as you stroke.

4. Upper Leaf. Paint the upper half of the banana leaf in the same way. Outline the outside shape first, then pull your strokes in toward the stem.

5. Stem. Pull a stem from tip to base to clean up the inside edges and re-establish the shape of the stem.

Palm Fronds

6

7

6. *Palm Frond Stem.* Double load a 1-inch (25mm) flat with Butter Pecan and Inca Gold Metallic. Pick up a little Wicker White on the Gold side. Pull a long curving stem downward that overlaps the banana leaf (see the finished design below for placement). Begin pulling long narrow leaves downward from the stem.

7. *Palm Leaves.* Continue adding more long slender leaves, letting some of them cross over in front of each other for a natural windblown look.

8. *Complete the Design.* Finish the palm frond by pulling long, slender leaves from the other side of the stem. Add more palm fronds and banana leaves on your cabinet front, sides and top wherever you would like them to be, but keep the design light and airy for the best effect. Pick up Inca Gold Metallic and Butter Pecan randomly as you paint for good shading and color variation. Let the paint dry, then spray with an exterior-grade lacquer and replace any knobs you removed.

At the Beach

Brushes
3⁄4-inch (19mm) flat
1-inch (25mm) flat
no. 16 flat
1⁄2-inch (13mm) rake
no. 4 fan

Surface
Two 18 x 24-inch (.46 x .69m) stretched canvases, with 1-1/2 inch (3.8 cm) thick, staple-free edges, by Fredrix Creative Edge

Additional Supplies
FolkArt Sponge Painters
FolkArt Flow Medium

*A*rtwork painted on canvas is no longer limited to indoor use only. Now you can display your paintings gallery-style anywhere you have wall space out of doors. Have a blank brick wall on your back porch that could use something colorful? These vibrant tropical paintings would be just the thing to brighten up a plain expanse of wall and remind you of warm summer days at the beach. Painting landscapes on canvas is easy—I used sponge painters to block in the large areas of sea, sky and sandy beach, and large flat brushes for the trees, foliage and flowers. For a fun and updated look, use two canvases placed side-by-side and carry the design across both. These canvases have smooth finished edges so you can paint the sides as well. No frames are needed!

FOLKART OUTDOOR DIMENSIONALS

Fresh Foliage Lemon Custard

FOLKART OUTDOOR OPAQUES

Butter Pecan | Wicker White | Cobalt Blue | Periwinkle | Fresh Foliage

Aqua | Raw Sienna | Burnt Umber | Hauser Dark Green | Thicket

Magenta | Pure Orange | Yellow Light | School Bus Yellow | Engine Red

Sky, Water and Beach

1. Horizon and Beach. Place the two canvases close together. Lightly pencil in a horizon line two-thirds of the way up on the canvases, and draw a line for the angle of the beach. Dampen a sponge painter and pick up Butter Pecan and Wicker White. Place in the sandy beach with long smooth strokes, continuing around the side and bottom edges of the canvases.

2. Sky. Sponge on the sky with Cobalt Blue and lots of Wicker White. Continue the sky around the top and side edges of the canvases.

3. Clouds. Pick up Wicker White on the same sponge and place puffy white clouds randomly in the sky using the rounded end of the sponge.

4. Distant Hills. Place a distant landmass on the left with Periwinkle thinned with Flow Medium, and on the right side with thinned Fresh Foliage and Aqua.

5. Distant Water. Begin the distant water with Cobalt Blue thinned with Flow Medium plus Wicker White, using the flat side of the sponge to establish the horizon line. Make smooth horizontal strokes; don't overblend.

6. Shallow Water. With the same dirty sponge, pick up more Wicker White and Aqua and paint the shallower water in the mid- and foreground. Pick up more Aqua sometimes and more Cobalt Blue other times to indicate shallower and deeper water.

Sand, Waves and Palm Trees

7. Island and Beach Sand. Paint the distant island on the right with Raw Sienna, Fresh Foliage, and Aqua on a 1-inch (25mm) flat. Shade the foreground beach with Butter Pecan thinned with Flow Medium. Spatter Burnt Umber on the sand with a no. 4 fan brush that you tap hard against the handle of another brush. This adds a sandy-looking texture to the beach.

8. Waves. With Wicker White and Flow Medium on a 1-inch (25mm) flat, use uneven, lateral stroking motions to paint foamy waves in the very shallow water next to the beach.

9. Water's Edge and Whitecaps. With the same brush, pick up Wicker White on the chisel edge and paint the edge of the water where it meets the sand, using random wiggle motions. Load

Wicker White on a no. 4 fan brush and tap on the large whitecaps on the foreground waves.

10. Background Foliage. Add texture in the area behind the palm trees, foliage and foreground flowers by sponging on Aqua and Fresh Foliage thinned with Flow Medium.

11. Palm Tree Trunks. Place in the palm trunks with Raw Sienna and Aqua plus a little bit of Burnt Umber on a no. 16 flat, stroking across to create the rough-textured bark.

12. Background Palm Fronds. The palm fronds on the background trees are painted with Hauser Dark Green, Fresh Foliage and Aqua on a 1/2-inch (13mm) rake brush.

Palm Trees and Tropical Flowers

13. Foreground Palm Trees. The large foreground palm trees on the left side of the design are painted with Hauser Dark Green, Fresh Foliage and Cobalt on a 1/2-inch (13mm) rake brush. Pick up Wicker White to highlight some of the tops of the fronds here and on the background palms.

14. Distant Palm Trees. The palm trees in the far distance on the right side are lightly brushed in with Fresh Foliage, Aqua and Raw Sienna on a 1/2-inch (13mm) rake brush.

15. Foreground Leaves and Filler Flowers. Paint the large leaves for the flowers in the foreground with Aqua, Fresh Foliage and Thicket on the outside edge. Pull stems into the leaves using the chisel edge. The little pink and orange filler flowers are Magenta and Pure Orange thinned with Flow Medium.

16. Blue Flowers. The bright blue flowers in the lower left of the canvas are painted with Cobalt Blue and Wicker White double loaded on a 3/4-inch (19mm) flat. Paint five ruffled-petal segments. Chisel in some Yellow Light strokes radiating out from the centers. Dot on centers of Fresh Foliage Dimensional paint.

17. Red Hibiscus. Double load a 1-inch (25mm) flat with School Bus Yellow and Engine Red. Paint each large petal with a ruffled top edge. Keep the Engine Red to the outside.

18. Hibiscus Centers. Draw detail lines radiating out from the center with Lemon Custard Outdoor Dimensional paint.

19. Stamens. Add the stamens with Fresh Foliage Outdoor Dimensional paint and dot on the pollen with Lemon Custard Dimensional.

20. Sideview Hibiscus. Double load a no. 16 flat with Engine Red and Yellow Light. Begin with the back petals and use ruffled-edge petal strokes. Keep the yellow to the outside.

21. Stamens. Paint the front two petals and enhance the ruffled edge with Lemon Custard Dimensional paint. Add a Fresh Foliage stamen and Lemon Custard pollen dots.

22. Orange Hibiscus. Double load a 1-inch (25mm) flat with School Bus Yellow and Engine Red and paint the large foreground hibiscus next to the blue flowers, and the orange sideview hibiscus behind. Detail the centers as you did for the red hibiscus.

Magnolias Outdoor Clock

Brushes
3/4-inch (19mm) flat
nos. 2 and 10 flats
no. 2 script liner

Surface
Large round clock with
bronze finish metal frame,
from Target

Additional Supplies
FolkArt Floating Medium

A beautifully painted clock such as this one can make a strong decorative statement in areas such as covered porches, sunrooms and patios. The design is simple—just some pink magnolia blossoms and a little brown sparrow—but the large size and bronze-toned metal frame of the clock make it a memorable and impressive accessory for your outdoor decor. Because the clock face is protected under glass, you can use regular acrylic paints, but I would keep it out of direct sunlight to prevent heat buildup behind the glass. Also, the delicate colors of the flowers will show up better if it's not in the glare of bright sunlight. If you don't have room for a large clock such as this one, a smaller round one will work just as well—just reduce the overall size of the design or cut back on the number of magnolia blossoms you paint.

FOLKART ACRYLICS

Burnt Umber   Wicker White   Berry Wine

12. *Final Petal Layer.* Add the final two petals to the light pink open magnolia, then attach the blossom to the branch with chisel edge strokes of Burnt Umber and Wicker White.

13. *Largest Magnolia.* The final dark pink magnolia blossom is at the 4 o'clock position on the clockface. Start with two dark pink back petals: keep the Berry Wine to the outside. Work a little more Wicker White into the brush and paint the lighter petal in front.

14. *Side Petals.* Turn your brush so the Berry Wine is to the outside and add two hanging petals at either side of the back petals.

15. *Final Magnolia Petal.* Paint a dark pink upright petal in

front to complete the blossom. Load a no. 2 script liner with inky Berry Wine and paint the detail lines at the base of the petals to shade them. Finish with a stem of Burnt Umber and Wicker White.

16. *Bird's Head and Back.* The little brown sparrow is painted entirely with Burnt Umber and Wicker White double loaded on a no. 10 flat. Use a half-circle stroke for the head and a long, smooth stroke for the back.

17. *Cheek and Belly.* With the same colors and brush, turn the brush so the Wicker White is on the outside edge. Paint the cheek and belly with short choppy strokes pulled out to the end to get a feathery effect.

Magnolias Outdoor Clock

Brushes
3/4-inch (19mm) flat
nos. 2 and 10 flats
no. 2 script liner

Surface
Large round clock with
bronze finish metal frame,
from Target

Additional Supplies
FolkArt Floating Medium

 A beautifully painted clock such as this one can make a strong decorative statement in areas such as covered porches, sunrooms and patios. The design is simple—just some pink magnolia blossoms and a little brown sparrow—but the large size and bronze-toned metal frame of the clock make it a memorable and impressive accessory for your outdoor decor. Because the clock face is protected under glass, you can use regular acrylic paints, but I would keep it out of direct sunlight to prevent heat buildup behind the glass. Also, the delicate colors of the flowers will show up better if it's not in the glare of bright sunlight. If you don't have room for a large clock such as this one, a smaller round one will work just as well—just reduce the overall size of the design or cut back on the number of magnolia blossoms you paint.

FOLKART ACRYLICS

Burnt Umber	Wicker White	Berry Wine

61

Branches and Magnolia Petals

1

2

3

4

5

1. Branches. Double load a 3/4-inch (19mm) flat with Burnt Umber and Wicker White. Stay up on the chisel edge and paint the magnolia tree branches within the circle of the round clock face for placement of the design. Here we're painting on a plain surface so the design is easy to see and you're not distracted by the clock's numbers and gauges.

2. Magnolia Bud. Double load a 3/4-inch (19mm) flat with Berry Wine and Wicker White. Paint the back two petals of the flower bud, keeping Wicker White to the outside. Start with the side petal, then lay the upright petal over it. These petals are painted similarly to a wiggle-edge leaf.

3. Magnolia Bud. Flip the brush so the Berry Wine side is to the outside, and paint the back side of the bud's front petal. The contrast between the darker pink and the light pink brings this petal to the front.

4. Opening Blossom. On the opening blossom located beneath the bud you just painted, start with the back two petals. Double load a 3/4-inch (19mm) flat with Berry Wine and Wicker White. Keep the Wicker White to the outside.

5. Middle Petals. Using the same brush and colors, paint the next layer of three petals; start these petals lower so you can still see the tops of the back petals. Pick up more Wicker White to create the lightest edges on some of the petals.

Ask Donna

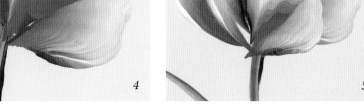

Q: When you paint flowers, where do you get your ideas? What are you inspired by?

A: When I'm looking for a new flower to paint, I study the photos in floral reference books, gardening magazines and seed catalogs. Sometimes I take my own pictures with a digital camera to get closeups of the flowers as well as the leaves. Most of the time when I paint a flower, I am going for an effect rather than trying to make it anatomically perfect in every detail. I prefer to work from a picture rather than an actual flower. This is because a picture is flat and one dimensional, and so is a painting. I use color, highlighting and shading all in one stroke to differentiate one petal or layer from another instead of mixing lots of colors.

6. Turned-edge Petal. In front of the petals you just painted in Step 5, paint a petal with one turned or curled edge. Using the same brush and colors and keeping the Wicker White to the outside, paint the first half of the petal, wiggling and sliding up to the tip. As you slide back down the other half, pivot your brush to the left to bring the white side of the brush over and across the front.

7. Drooping Petal. Finish with a petal that droops off to the right side. Attach the blossom to the branch with Burnt Umber and Wicker White chisel-edge strokes.

8. Detail Lines. Detail the magnolia petals and deepen the shading at the base of the petals with inky Berry Wine on a no. 2 script liner.

9. Dark Pink Magnolia. The dark pink magnolia, located at the bottom of the clockface below the bird, is painted the same way as the blossom you just painted. To get the dark pink color, keep the Berry Wine side of the brush to the outside edges of the petals.

10. Fully Open Magnolia. To begin the fully open light pink magnolia to the right of the dark pink one, double load a 3/4-inch (19mm) flat with Berry Wine and Wicker White and start with the two back petals. Keep the Wicker White side of the brush to the outside. Add a curled petal to the left. Paint the back half of the petal first, then overlap it with a smooth horizontal stroke from base to tip, keeping the Wicker White to the top edge of the petal.

11. Middle Petals. Add another layer of two more petals to the right, one laying sideways and one more upright.

12. *Final Petal Layer.* Add the final two petals to the light pink open magnolia, then attach the blossom to the branch with chisel edge strokes of Burnt Umber and Wicker White.

13. *Largest Magnolia.* The final dark pink magnolia blossom is at the 4 o'clock position on the clockface. Start with two dark pink back petals: keep the Berry Wine to the outside. Work a little more Wicker White into the brush and paint the lighter petal in front.

14. *Side Petals.* Turn your brush so the Berry Wine is to the outside and add two hanging petals at either side of the back petals.

15. *Final Magnolia Petal.* Paint a dark pink upright petal in

front to complete the blossom. Load a no. 2 script liner with inky Berry Wine and paint the detail lines at the base of the petals to shade them. Finish with a stem of Burnt Umber and Wicker White.

16. *Bird's Head and Back.* The little brown sparrow is painted entirely with Burnt Umber and Wicker White double loaded on a no. 10 flat. Use a half-circle stroke for the head and a long, smooth stroke for the back.

17. *Cheek and Belly.* With the same colors and brush, turn the brush so the Wicker White is on the outside edge. Paint the cheek and belly with short choppy strokes pulled out to the end to get a feathery effect.

18. *Tail Feathers.* Paint the tail feathers starting with the longest one and tapering down on both sides. Don't curve these strokes; keep them straight. Tail feathers are always straight.

19. *Wing.* Add a few more shorter feathers to the tail. Stroke the wing with one smooth motion from neck to tail, keeping the Burnt Umber to the top.

20. *Wing Feathers.* Pull short chisel-edge strokes of Burnt Umber starting at the outside edge and layering inward.

21. *Feet, Eye and Beak.* Load a no. 2 script liner with inky Burnt Umber and paint short curving lines for the feet. Double load a no. 2 flat with Burnt Umber and Wicker White and work in a lighter brown where the eyes are. Add the beak with the Burnt Umber side of the brush. With a no. 2 script liner add the eye with Burnt Umber. Add highlights to the eye, face and beak with Wicker White on a no. 2 script liner.

For the Gardener

Brushes for Paper
nos. 6, 8, 12, 16 flats
no. 2 script liner
1/2-inch (13mm) scruffy

Surfaces
Straw hat from discount store

Brushed leather gloves from home center

Basket tote with cloth liner from craft supply store

*W*hat better way to have fun in the garden than to dress the part! A flower-bedecked straw hat will keep the sun off your head. Soft and resilient brushed leather gloves will keep your hands clean. And a pretty painted tote basket lets you carry all your freshly cut flowers into the house for arranging. Even if you're not a gardener yourself, you probably know someone who is, and wouldn't this make a lovely gift for her? Since these surfaces have a lot of texture, I recommend using the FolkArt Brushes for Paper. They have stiffer bristles than acrylics brushes, which makes paint application easy.

FOLKART OUTDOOR DIMENSIONALS

Lemon Custard	Fresh Foliage

FOLKART OUTDOOR OPAQUES

Pure Orange	Engine Red	Cobalt Blue	Wicker White

Green Forest	Fresh Foliage	Yellow Light

Gardening Gloves

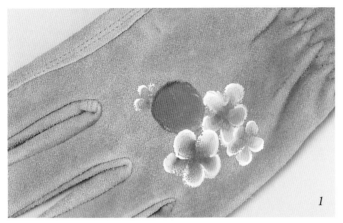

1. Orange and Blue Flowers. Load a no. 8 flat into Pure Orange and sideload in Yellow Light. Paint circles for the orange flower. Load a no. 6 flat into Cobalt Blue and sideload in Wicker White. Paint the five-petal flowers, keeping the Wicker White to the outside. You may need to overstroke several times to get good coverage on the textured surface like these brushed-leather gloves.

2. Flower Centers. Double load a no. 6 flat with Yellow Light and some Wicker White and place the center of the orange flower. Dot on the centers of the blue flowers with Lemon Custard Outdoor Dimensional paint.

3. Orange Flower Petals. Outline the orange flower with Yellow Light on a no. 2 script liner. Detail the petals with Pure Orange sideloaded with Yellow Light on a no. 6 flat. Make sure the orange part of the flower is dry before adding the petal detail.

4. Leaves. Double load Green Forest and Fresh Foliage on a no. 6 flat and paint the little one-stroke leaves. The smallest green leaves are Fresh Foliage on the tip of the brush. With Fresh Foliage and Green Forest on a no. 2 script liner, dot around the center of the orange flower. Finish with a dark green tendril.

Straw Hat

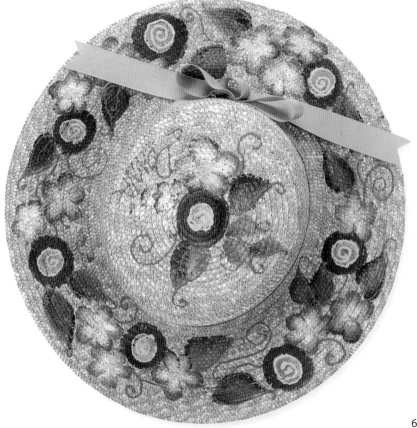

1. *Orange Flowers.* Base the orange flowers with circles of Pure Orange, sideloaded into Engine Red, using a no. 16 flat brush for paper.

2. *Blue Five-petal Flowers.* Double load Cobalt Blue and Wicker White on a no. 12 flat. Load heavily for the textured straw. Keep the Cobalt Blue to the outside and paint clusters of five-petal flowers.

3. *Leaves.* Add one-stroke leaves with Green Forest and Fresh Foliage on a no. 16 flat. Fill in the centers of the leaves if needed since the straw hat is so textured.

4. *Blue Flower Centers.* Double load a 1/2-inch (13mm) scruffy with Yellow Light and Fresh Foliage and pounce on the centers of the orange flowers. Dot Lemon Custard Outdoor Dimensional on the blue flowers' centers using the tip of the bottle.

5. *Tendrils and Spirals.* With Fresh Foliage Outdoor Dimensional, add tendrils using the pointed tip of the bottle. With Lemon Custard Dimensional, draw spirals in the orange flower centers.

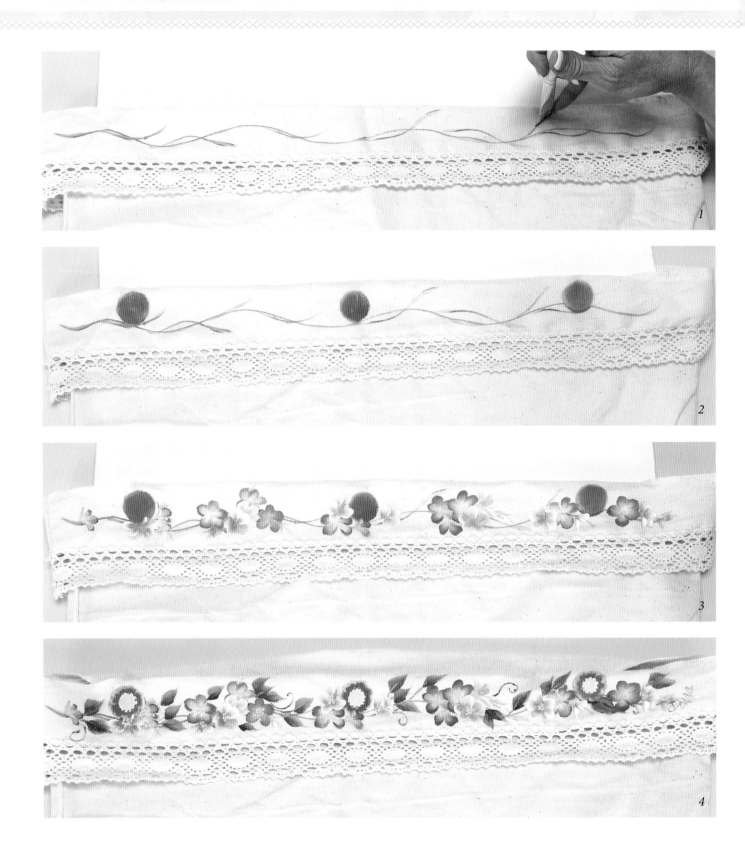

1. *Vine.* Place a sturdy piece of cardboard in the opening of the cloth liner so you will have a smooth surface to support your painting area. Using the chisel edge of a no. 16 flat brush for paper, paint a curving vine with Green Forest and Fresh Foliage.

2. *Orange Flowers.* Load a no. 12 flat with Pure Orange and sideload into Yellow Light. Block in circles for the orange flowers.

3. *Blue Flowers.* Load a no. 8 flat with Cobalt Blue and sideload into Wicker White. Paint the blue five-petal flowers. Flip your brush so the Wicker White is to the outside on some flowers and the Cobalt Blue is outside on others. This gives you a variety of darker blue and lighter blue flowers along the vine.

4. *Floral Details and Leaves.* Paint the centers of the orange flowers with Yellow Light and Wicker White. Dot the centers of the blue flowers with Lemon Custard Outdoor Dimensional. Add leaves with Green Forest and Fresh Foliage double loaded on a no. 8 flat. Detail the orange flowers with little loopy petals of Pure Orange and Yellow Light. Shade the centers with dots of Green Forest and Fresh Foliage on a no. 2 script liner, and then pull a few tendrils here and there along the vine. After all the paint is thoroughly dry, you can hand-launder your basket liner in warm water and hang it to dry. Place it back in the basket to reshape it.

Evening Lights

Enamels Brushes
nos. 8, 10, 12 flats
1/8-inch (3mm) scruffy
no. 2 script liner

Surfaces
Tall and short drinking glasses
available from any home store

Additional Supplies
Dip 'n Etch by EtchAll,
available at any craft
supply store

Sturdy disposable plastic
container

*W*hen the sun dips low in the sky and the cool breezes of evening signal the end of the day, you can add a relaxing glow to your patio or porch with these pretty little votive candle holders. These are so simple and inexpensive to paint, you may want to set dozens of them along the railing of your back deck. Place fine white sand in the bottom of each glass for weight and stability and to absorb the melting candlewax. I used regular drinking glasses bought at a home store and gave them a frosted finish, or you can buy already-frosted glasses. Paint a simple flower on each one and light up the evening!

FOLKART ENAMELS

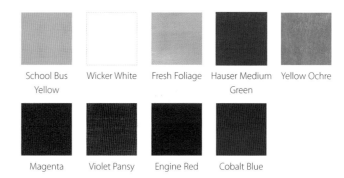

School Bus Yellow   Wicker White   Fresh Foliage   Hauser Medium Green   Yellow Ochre

Magenta   Violet Pansy   Engine Red   Cobalt Blue

Frosting the Glasses

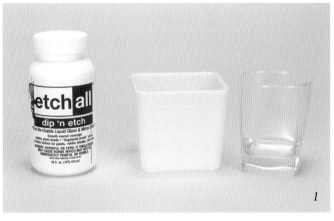

1

2

3

4

5

6

1. Materials Needed. If you want to frost the outside of your glasses before painting on them, here's an easy and inexpensive way to do it. Purchase a jar of EtchAll Dip 'n Etch at any craft store, and gather up a sturdy plastic container and the glasses you want to frost.

2. Determine Etch Line. Fill the plastic container halfway with water and place the glass down in. Use weights such as marbles or stones in the glass to keep it from floating. Add or remove water until the waterline is where you want the top of the frosted area on the glass to be. Leave about one inch (25mm) at the top clear.

3. Mark Etch Line. Remove the glass. Mark the outside of the container with a line that's level with the height of the water.

4. Add Dip 'n Etch. Remove the water and dry the container. Fill it with Dip 'n Etch up to the level line you marked on the outside.

5. Place in Dip 'n Etch. Place the weighted glass down in the Dip 'n Etch and leave it there for 15 minutes.

6. Rinse and Dry. Remove the glass from the etching solution, rinse under running water and dry thoroughly. Pour the Dip 'n Etch back into its jar—it can be reused over and over.

Yellow and White Squash Blossom

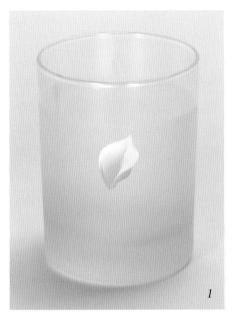

1. First Petal. Double load a no. 12 flat Enamels brush with School Bus Yellow and Wicker White. Paint the first petal by sliding smoothly up to the tip, and sliding smoothly back down. Keep the Wicker White to the outside.

2. Four More Petals. Add four more ruffled-edge petals to complete the flower. Turn the glass to make painting each petal easier and make sure the Wicker White side of the brush is always to the outside edge of each petal.

3. Stem. Add a branching stem coming from the back of the blossom with Fresh Foliage and Hauser Medium Green on a no. 10 flat Enamels brush.

4. Center. Pick up a little Yellow Ochre on the chisel edge of the no. 10 flat and add fine lines radiating up and outward from the center for shading and depth. Dot Fresh Foliage in the center for a stamen. Let the paint dry for 24 hours before using the glass.

Pink Coneflower

1. Petals. Double load a no. 8 flat Enamels brush with a little Magenta and a lot of Wicker White. Begin the coneflower petals using a daisy petal stroke. Start at the outside edge and pull each petal in toward the center, lifting to the chisel edge to form a point.

2. Layer Petals. Add more petals to the first layer, then add a second layer of shorter petals on top of the first. This is a sideview flower so you will not be painting a complete circle of petals like a daisy.

3. Center. Double load Yellow Ochre and School Bus Yellow on a 1/8-inch (3mm) Enamels scruffy and pounce on the coneflower center. Highlight with a little Wicker White on the top.

4. Stem. Add a chisel-edge stem with Fresh Foliage and Hauser Medium Green double loaded on the no. 8 flat. Let the paint dry for 24 hours before using the glass.

1

2

3

4

Lavender

1

2

3

1. Petals. Double load Violet Pansy and Wicker White on a no. 8 flat Enamels brush and pull some chisel-edge petal strokes that angle down toward the stem.

2. Layer Petals. Pull more petals along the sides to fill in the layers. As you reload the brush, pick up more Violet Pansy sometimes and more Wicker White other times to vary the petal colors and add depth and roundness to the lavender blossom.

3. Stem and Leaves. Double load the no. 8 flat with Fresh Foliage and Hauser Medium Green and pull a curving stem, leading with the lighter green. Add little leaves with the same brush and colors, using a chisel-edge petal stroke. Let the paint dry for 24 hours before using the glass.

Ask Donna

Q: What is your favorite flower to paint? Why? What does it mean to you?

A: My current favorite flower was not always my favorite, either to paint, pick, or grow. Now it has become all three. It is the rose. The one-stroke rose is also known as my "signature flower." People in the painting world easily recognize my rose. Whenever I am painting a demonstration the rose is always requested. What makes it my favorite now? Its versatility. I haven't found a surface yet that can't have a rose painted on it. Roses also come in almost every color and shade so they can be painted to work with any decor. In this book, you'll find several roses on very different surfaces—and they all work! Check out the roses on the Spring Address Sign on page 32, the tall Butterfly House on page 42, and the stylized folk art rose on the Terra Cotta Wall Planter on page 98.

Daylily

1. Petal. Double load School Bus Yellow and Engine Red on a no. 8 flat Enamels brush and paint a long, pointed petal. Start on the chisel edge at the base, push down on the bristles to widen the center part, then lift back up to the chisel and slide to the tip. Slide back down the other side without turning or pivoting the brush.

2. Blossom. Fill out the daylily blossom with four more petals, keeping the Engine Red to the outside for all. Turn the glass as you work to make painting easier. Make sure the outside tip on each petal is a sharp, distinct point.

3. Stamens. Load a no. 8 flat with Fresh Foliage and use the chisel edge to paint the stamens, stroking them inward toward the center. Shade the center with Hauser Medium Green, and touch on pollen dots with Wicker White.

4. Stem. Pull a stem with Fresh Foliage and Hauser Medium Green on the chisel edge of the no. 8 flat. Let the paint dry for 24 hours before using the glass.

1

2

3

4

Blue Wildflower

1. Petals. Double load a no. 8 flat Enamels brush with Cobalt Blue and Wicker White and touch on the little petals with the chisel edge of the brush.

2. Stemlets. Load a no. 2 script liner with Hauser Medium Green and pull little stemlets from the petals by grabbing the bottom of the petal and pulling downward in a slight curve. Keep these stemlets very thin and delicate.

3. Main Stem and Leaves. The main stem is Fresh Foliage and Hauser Medium Green double loaded on a no. 8 flat. Lead with the lighter green. Pull long, slender leaves out from the stem with the chisel edge. Let the paint dry for 24 hours before using the glass.

Pillows for the Porch

Brushes for Paper
nos. 2, 10 and 12 flats
3/4-inch (19mm) flat
no. 2 script liner

Surface
Donna Dewberry's Quilting
Basics fabrics in the crackle
design

14-inch (35.6cm) square
pillow forms stuffed with
polyester batting

Additional Supplies
FolkArt Floating Medium

I love to sit outside on my front porch on a comfy wicker chair or, if the grandkids make room for me, on our old-fashioned porch swing. Pillows always add a comforting touch to outdoor furniture, and colorful pillows like these give freshness and liveliness to any porch. The bright blues, greens and yellows of these three pillows work well with almost any home decor colors. I painted these designs on my own Quilting Basics fabric, which can be found in craft and sewing stores. Painting on fabric is easy with the FolkArt Brushes for Paper. Be sure your paint is dry before you sew your pillow together. If you're not into sewing, buy a plain square pillow in a color such as taupe or light yellow.

FOLKART ACRYLICS

Cobalt Blue

Wicker White

Thicket

Fresh Foliage

Yellow Light

Yellow Ochre

Pillow with Blue Leaves

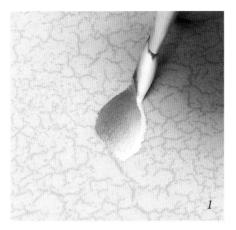  

1. *One-Stroke Leaf.* Double load a no. 12 flat brush for paper with Cobalt Blue and Wicker White, then dip into Floating Medium. Paint a one stroke leaf, following the instructions on page 16.

2. *Side Leaves and Stems.* Add two more one-stroke leaves on either side of your first one. Pull chisel edge stems partway into each leaf. Join the stems at the bottom to form a three-leaf cluster.

3. *Leaf Clusters.* Also paint four-leaf clusters here and there for variety. As you reload your brush, pick up more Cobalt Blue sometimes for darker blue leaves. Other times, pick up more Wicker White for lighter blue leaves.

4. *Scattered Leaves.* To make the most interesting design on your pillow, add more three- and four-leaf clusters, turning them in different directions and making them different shapes. But keep the spacing between them pretty consistent so the design looks neat and well-planned.

Pillow with Ferns and Butterflies

1

2

3

4

1. Fern Stems and Leaves. Double load Thicket and Fresh Foliage on a no. 12 flat brush for paper, and place curving fern stems. Paint the fern leaves the same as little one-stroke leaves, but stay up on the chisel edge more. Alternate picking up more Thicket or more Fresh Foliage to vary the leaf colors.

2. Blue Butterfly Wings. Paint the wings of the butterfly with Cobalt Blue and Wicker White double loaded on a no. 12 flat. Keep the Cobalt Blue to the outside.

3. Butterfly Body. The body is painted with Fresh Foliage on a no. 2 flat sideloaded into Thicket. Use little C-strokes to make the segments. The antennae are painted with inky Thicket on a no. 2 script liner.

4. Wing Details. Detail the wings with long comma strokes of Yellow Light and highlight with shorter commas of Wicker White using the no. 2 flat. The sideview butterflies on the pillow are painted with the same brushes and colors.

Pillow with Blue Flowers

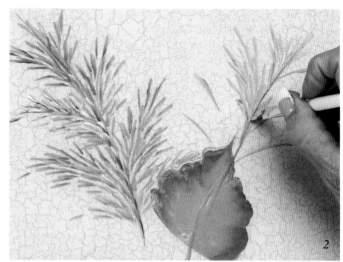

1. Stems and Large Leaves. Place the fern stems with Thicket and Fresh Foliage double loaded on a 3⁄4-inch (19mm) flat. Paint the big leaves with the same brush and colors.

2. Ferns. Double load a no. 12 flat with Thicket and Fresh Foliage. Paint the fern stemlets and tiny leaves with little chisel-edge strokes that you touch and pull lightly.

3. Blue Flowers. Double load a no. 12 flat with Cobalt Blue and Wicker White and paint florets of ruffled-edge petals to establish the shape. This is the first and innermost layer of petals. Pick up more Wicker White each time you load the brush and keep it to the outside edges of the petals.

4. Darker Blue Flowers. Fill in with another layer of florets, but this time, flip the brush so the Cobalt Blue is to the outside. Each time you reload the brush, pick up more Cobalt Blue.

5. Lighter Blue Flowers. For the final layer of petals, flip the brush again so the Wicker White is to the outside. Pick up more Wicker White each time you reload. Paint a few more florets but don't cover up the previous layers.

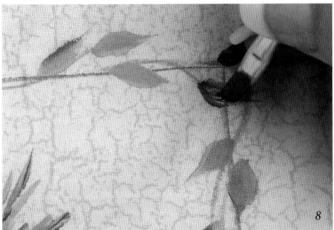

6. *Flower Centers.* Use a no. 2 script liner to add small vein lines of inky Cobalt Blue to shade the centers. Dot the centers with Yellow Ochre and Yellow Light on the end of the brush handle.

7. *Border.* Load a no. 12 flat with Cobalt Blue and chisel-edge a straight line to start the border around all four sides of the design.

8. *Blue Leaves.* Paint little one-stroke leaves winding back and forth over the straight borderline, using Cobalt Blue and Wicker White on a no. 10 flat.

9. *Butterfly.* Double load a no. 10 flat with Yellow Light and Wicker White. Paint the two larger wings using the one-stroke leaf technique, then two chisel strokes coming up from the bottom for the lower wings. Use inky Thicket on a no. 2 script liner for the body and antennae.

Wildflower Planter

Enamels Brushes
nos. 2, 6, 8 and 12 flats
no. 2 script liner

Surface
Enameled metal planter with
handles, available at Target

Additional Supplies
FolkArt Clear Medium

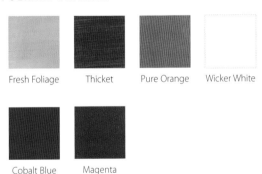

*P*lanters come in all shapes, sizes and materials, but the ones I like to paint on most are the sturdy metal ones with a smooth enameled finish. Because the surface is slick and nonporous, I use the Enamels paints and brushes to make painting quick and easy. For this project I painted some simple wildflowers dancing around the sides of the planter. The design is simple and airy, and won't detract from the flowers that are planted inside. I suggest placing potted plants in the planter rather than filling it with soil. That way you don't have to drill drainage holes in the bottom and you can change out your plants as the seasons change.

FOLKART ENAMELS

Fresh Foliage	Thicket	Pure Orange	Wicker White

Cobalt Blue	Magenta

Orange Trumpet Flowers

1. Stems and Leaves. Paint the main stems and branches with a no. 12 flat double loaded with Fresh Foliage and Thicket. Add long, slender leaves—not too many, leave room for the flowers.

2. Trumpet Flowers. Paint the backs of the trumpets with Pure Orange and Wicker White double loaded on a no. 8 flat. These are tight little C-strokes, with the Wicker White at the base.

3. Ruffled Edges. Ruffle the back of the trumpet keeping the Wicker White to the top of the trumpet.

4. Front Petals. Add the front part of the trumpet with the Wicker White to the top of the ruffled edge. Paint this part of the trumpet lower so you can still see the back petal. This is what makes the trumpet seem rounded and open at the top.

Ask Donna

Q: What is an inexpensive way to include painted items in my garden or yard?

A: A common saying in the decorative painting world is, "If it doesn't move, paint it!" What this means to me is that almost any surface is fair game (except for husbands napping in their recliners). You just have to take into consideration how the surface will be used. Start with some objects that are looking a little worn out; if you don't want to discard them, then a little paint might just be the answer. Here are some possible surfaces I'm sure you have laying around: Lawn chairs and chaise lounges, tables, patio umbrellas, terra cotta pots, landscape bricks or lumber, doors and fence support posts. See what I mean? You might have to clean them off or spray them with a basecoat first, but painting a few flowers or leaves on them will give them new life and will get your garden blooming even if the plants aren't.

Blue Flowers and Magenta Buds

1. Stems and Leaves. Paint a thin stem and branches with Thicket on the chisel edge of a no. 8 flat. Load a no. 2 flat with Thicket and lots of Wicker White and paint tiny one-stroke leaves.

2. Blue Flowers. Double load a no. 6 flat with Cobalt Blue and Wicker White and begin painting little chisel-stroke petals, pulling each petal toward the stem and leading with the Wicker White.

3. Vary the Blues. Finish the blue flower with lots of chisel-edge petal strokes overlapping the first layer. Flip your brush so the Cobalt Blue leads for some darker blue petals here and there. Attach the stems to the bottoms of the blue flowers.

4. Magenta Flower Stems. Double load Fresh Foliage and Thicket on a no. 8 flat and paint the main stems and branching stems, then the little stemlets at the ends.

5. Magenta Buds. Double load Magenta plus a little Wicker White on a no. 6 flat. Dab on little buds at the ends of the stemlets using the chisel edge of the brush.

6. Leaves. Double load a no. 8 flat with Fresh Foliage and Thicket and paint slender little leaves along the main stems.

7. White Butterflies. Finish with little white butterflies hovering over the wildflowers. These have Wicker White wings and Thicket bodies and antennae.

Garden Tools Mailbox

Enamels Brushes
3/4-inch (19mm) flat
no. 12 flat
nos. 1 and 2 script liners

Surface
White enameled rural
mailbox from a home
improvement center

Additional Supplies
FolkArt Flow Medium

*H*ave you ever walked out to the yard ready to do some serious gardening, and then realized you left your pruners in the garage? Here's a great way to keep your garden tools handy just where you need them—in the garden! This is a standard rural mailbox which can be found at any home improvement store. I just repurposed it as a small storage container for my most-used gardening tools. Now I don't have to run back and forth gathering up what I need. I painted this with brightly colored pots and added quiet green ferns and a couple of shimmery dragonflies. It looks right at home in my garden.

FOLKART OUTDOOR METALLICS

Metallic Blue   Metallic Emerald
Sapphire   Green

FOLKART OUTDOOR OPAQUES

Soft Apple   Yellow Ochre   Lemon Custard   Engine Red   Thicket

Fresh Foliage   Wicker White   Barn Wood

Pots and Lacy Ferns

1. **Pots.** Use a ¾-inch (19mm) flat to basecoat the pots. The blue pot is Metallic Blue Sapphire. The green pot is Soft Apple shaded with Metallic Emerald Green. The rim is a series of curved strokes. The yellow bowl is Lemon Custard shaded with Yellow Ochre.

2. **Yellow Bowl.** Stripe the yellow bowl with Engine Red thinned with Flow Medium for the wide stripe and Metallic Sapphire Blue for the fine pinstripes. Outline the wide red stripe with straight (unthinned) Engine Red on a no. 2 script liner.

3. **Green Pot.** On the green pot, shade under the rim and paint a cluster of one-stroke leaves with Metallic Emerald Green.

4. **Lacy Fern Stems.** Place the fern stems in the blue pot with the chisel edge of a no. 12 flat double loaded with Thicket and Soft Apple. Let them extend out over the other two pots for a full look.

5. **Lacy Fern Leaves.** With the same brush and colors, add chisel edge strokes for the lacy fern leaves, angling them inward toward the stems. Keep these ferns light and airy so they'll contrast well with the other, more substantial ferns.

6. **Fern Fronds.** Let some of the fern fronds drape over the rim of the pot, and extend the tallest ones upward to the top of the mailbox.

Ferns and Dragonflies

7. *Wide Leaf Fern.* For the yellow bowl, the fern has wider leaves. Double load Fresh Foliage and Thicket on a no. 12 flat and paint pairs of leaves that are opposite each other on the stem.

8. *Stems.* Where the ferns overlap, pick up more Fresh Foliage on your brush so the ferns in front will show up better. As you finish the leaves on each stem, re-stroke the stem to clean it up. Finish with a curled stem or two using Fresh Foliage on a no. 1 script liner.

9. *Round Leaf Fern.* Place the fern stems in the green pot with Thicket on a no. 2 script liner. Double load a no. 12 flat with Thicket and Soft Apple and dab on the rounded fern leaves, pulling to a point where they atttach to the stems.

10. *Stems.* Fill out all the stems of this fern with more rounded leaves. Finish with some curling stems using Thicket on a no. 2 script liner.

11. *Dragonflies.* The wings are painted with Metallic Blue Sapphire and the body and antennae are Metallic Emerald Green.

12. *Shading.* Load a 3/4-inch (19mm) flat with Flow Medium and sideload into Barn Wood. Shade around and between the pots to make them look dimensional and lift them from the background. Shade underneath the ferns in the yellow bowl with a sideload float of Yellow Ochre.

Windowbox with Daylilies

Brushes
1-inch (25mm) flat
3/8-inch (10mm) angular

Surface
Homemade wooden windowbox, 36 inches (1m) long, 7 inches (17.8cm) high and 9 inches (22.9cm) wide. Holds five 6-inch pots.

*W*indowboxes are back in style! There are many kinds to choose from, such as lightweight resin foam, wrought iron "hayracks" and wooden ones like this, which was made for me by my talented husband. It's a simple rectangular box made from exterior grade plywood, dressed up with beadboard and trim molding and painted white. Since it is a large piece, I painted larger-than-life daylilies in brilliant colors. The size of the flowers makes it easier to paint them right over the grooves of the beadboard with a large flat brush. Daylilies come in many shades so choose the colors you like best.

FOLKART OUTDOOR DIMENSIONALS

Fresh Foliage

Lemon Custard

FOLKART OUTDOOR OPAQUES

Engine Red

Yellow Light

Fresh Foliage

School Bus Yellow

Yellow Ochre

Lemon Custard

Orange Daylilies

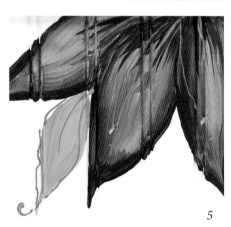

1. Orange Petals. Double load Engine Red and Yellow Light on a 1-inch (25mm) flat. Paint the large petals of the orange daylily, stroking downward toward the pointed tip. Keep the Engine Red to the outside. Refer to the finished windowbox at the bottom of the facing page for placement of the flowers.

2. Detail Lines and Leaf. Using a 3/8-inch (10mm) angular brush and Engine Red, pull streaks out from the flower center. Also clean up the edges of the petals, extending the pointed tips of the petals slightly. Add a green leaf with Fresh Foliage and School Bus Yellow double loaded on a l-inch (25mm) flat.

3. Veins. Pull a green vein down the center of each petal with Fresh Foliage, using the chisel edge of the flat brush.

4. Stamens. Use Fresh Foliage Outdoor Dimensional paint to draw stamens starting at the outside and pulling in toward the center.

5. Outlining. Use Fresh Foliage Outdoor Dimensional to outline the leaf. Add anthers to the tips of the stamens with Lemon Custard Outdoor Dimensional.

Ask Donna

Q: When you paint on items that will be displayed outdoors, what kind of paints and brushes do you use?

A: For most of these pieces I'm using FolkArt Outdoor paints. This paint has a sealer already in it. Another paint I use is the FolkArt Enamels paint, made for glass, ceramic, metal, and other smooth, nonporous surfaces. After the surface has dried overnight, it can be baked in a warm oven to cure the paint, which makes it washable. If you cannot find the Outdoor paints in your area and you are going to paint on a nonporous surface, then use the Enamels. If neither Outdoor nor Enamels paints are available to you, then use the acrylic paints. Keep in mind that the acrylics will not stay on glass or ceramics, and they will need to be sealed with several coats of spray lacquer if you use them on wood or metal.

Yellow Daylilies

6

7

8

9

6. Yellow Petals. Paint a leaf and stem with Fresh Foliage and School Bus Yellow double loaded on a 1-inch (25mm) flat. (Refer to the finished painting below for placement of leaves, stems and flowers.) Double load the flat with Yellow Ochre and Lemon Custard and paint the petals. Keep the Yellow Ochre to the outside.

7. Shade the Center. Pick up a tiny bit of Engine Red on the same flat brush you had loaded with Yellow Ochre and Lemon Custard

for step 6. Place the flower center with a U-stroke. Pull shading from the red center upward onto each petal.

8. Veins. Chisel on a Fresh Foliage vein in each petal and pull Fresh Foliage Dimensional stamens and Lemon Custard anthers. Outline the leaf with Fresh Foliage Dimensional.

9. Trim. Paint the trim with Fresh Foliage on a 1-inch (25mm) flat.

Terra Cotta Wall Planters

Brushes
nos. 10, 12 and 16 flats
no. 2 script liner

Surface
Terra cotta wall planters with
flat backs, available at garden
centers and craft stores

Additional Supplies
FolkArt Flow Medium

*H*ere's an easy way to add a hot and spicy Southwestern ambience to your outdoor areas. These terra cotta wall planters were painted with the bright red, yellow and ochre colors of the southwest desert and would look great planted with a few cactus or succulents native to the arid desert regions of the country. These wall planters have a flat side on the back so they can be hung flat against any wall—just make sure you bolt them securely to the wall so they will hold the weight of your plantings. These look best on an outside wall in groups of at least two. They come in many shapes, from half-moons like these to urn-shaped and cone shaped, which look wonderful stuffed with dried flowers and ornamental grasses.

FOLKART OUTDOOR OPAQUES

Pure Orange   Engine Red   Burnt Umber   School Bus Yellow   Berry Wine

Fresh Foliage   Thicket   Wicker White   Yellow Ochre

Rose Center and Petals

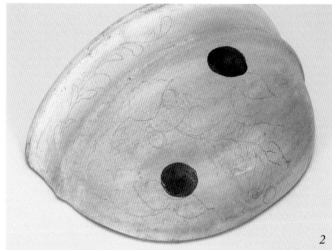

1. Pencil in Design. Draw the placement of your vines, leaves and roses on the terra cotta planter with a pencil. Check your design before you start painting. Paint can't be wiped off of terra cotta unless you've sealed it first.

2. Rose Centers. Double load Pure Orange and Engine Red on a no. 16 flat and pick up plenty of Flow Medium to help the paint go on more smoothly. Paint the rose centers with two half-circle strokes.

3. Rose Petals. With the same brush and colors, add two open rose petals using the one-stroke leaf motion.

4. Shade Throat. Load a no. 12 flat with Flow Medium and side-load into Burnt Umber. Paint a C-stroke to shade part of the throat of the rose center.

5. Highlight Throat. Come back in with the dirty brush sideloaded into School Bus Yellow and complete the throat with another C-stroke to highlight.

6. Comma Strokes. Use the chisel edge of a no. 12 flat loaded with School Bus Yellow and detail the two side petals with comma strokes. Paint a longer comma along the outside edges and a shorter one nested into the longer one.

5

6

Ask Donna

Q: How do you protect your painted terra cotta planters from the rain? How do you keep the colors from fading in the sun?

A: Terra cotta is very porous, and even if you seal the inside and outside, moisture will still find a way to be absorbed. The best thing to do to protect your painting is to seal the outside and use a plastic liner for the inside. This will allow any moisture to evaporate and not get trapped in the terra cotta under the painting. If moisture gets into the terra cotta it can cause the paint to bubble and peel.

Lacquer is the only sealer that I know of that does not turn amber or yellow in the sun. Many sealers say that they don't yellow, but after trying several I can tell you that they do. Lacquer will give added protection to the paint from fading, and it will protect the piece from moisture. A little fading can still occur over time, but it will be minimal if you use the Outdoor paints and then seal the entire piece with an exterior grade spray lacquer.

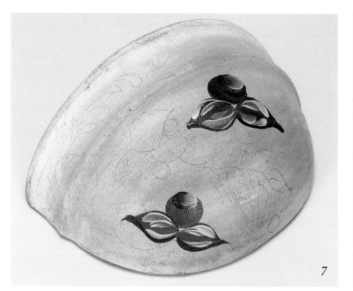

7. *Outline Roses.* Outlne the side petals and detail the bowl of the rose with Berry Wine on a no. 2 script liner.

8. *Stems and Small Leaves.* Double load a no. 16 flat with Fresh Foliage and Thicket and pull stems into the flowers. Paint comma strokes tucked in among the rose centers and side petals for small leaves. As you reload your brush, pick up more Fresh Foliage sometimes and more Thicket other times for leaf color variation.

9. *Large Leaves.* The large leaves have one ruffled-edge side and one layered-comma-stroke side. Double load Fresh Foliage and Thicket for the ruffled edge side. Pick up a little Wicker White for the layered-stroke side of the leaf.

10. *One-Stroke Leaves.* The lightest green comma strokes are painted with Fresh Foliage on a no. 12 flat. Add little dark green one-stroke leaves with Thicket on a no. 10 flat.

Berries and Comma Stroke Border

11. *Yellow Berries.* The yellow berries are painted with a no. 10 flat loaded with Yellow Ochre and sideloaded with Burnt Umber. Use two half-circle strokes to paint the berries. Shade them with Burnt Umber comma strokes.

12. *Comma Stroke Border.* Paint a border of comma strokes along the rim of the planter with a no. 12 flat double loaded with School Bus Yellow and Engine Red. Reload your brush often and pick up more red sometimes and more yellow other times to create color variation in the comma strokes.

Berry Pretty Wind Chimes

Brushes
nos. 2, 6, 8 and 10 flats
nos. 0 and 8/0 liners
nos. 1 and 2 script liners

Surface
Metal wind chimes available at garden stores and craft supply stores. These came painted black, but if yours are not, basecoat them inside and out with Licorice Outdoor Opaque paint.

*W*ind chimes are enjoyed by many for their soft bell-like songs when they move in a breeze. The sound can be very relaxing and if you hand-paint them with a colorful design, they can also add visual interest to your porch or deck. On this set of six bells, I painted a series of berries that might be enjoyed by the cute little bird cutout that came with my wind chimes. The two bells on the right have strawberries, the middle two bells have blueberries, and the two on the left have orange berries. They are all painted with Outdoor Opaque paints so they are well-protected from the weather.

FOLKART OUTDOOR OPAQUES

Burnt Umber Wicker White Fresh Foliage Thicket School Bus Yellow

Engine Red Cobalt Blue Pure Orange

Strawberries

1. *Bell #1 — Strawberry Vine.* Load a no. 2 script liner with Burnt Umber and stroke through Wicker White. Paint a wandering vine and branches around the bell. Double load Fresh Foliage and Thicket on a no. 8 flat and paint a variety of leaves coming off the main branches. Keep the Fresh Foilage to the outside so the leaves show up well against the black background.

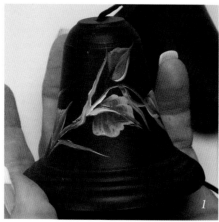

2. *Basecoat Strawberries.* Basecoat the strawberries with a little bit of Wicker White and School Bus Yellow. This will help your red color pop off the black background.

3. *Add Color.* The strawberries are School Bus Yellow sideloaded into Engine Red on a no. 6 flat. Keep the yellow to the inside so they look like ripening berries. Stroke downward from the stem to the tip.

4. *Seeds and Hulls.* Load Fresh Foliage and a touch of Thicket on an 8/0 liner and dot on the seeds. Paint the hulls with the same colors on a no. 2 flat. Attach the stems of the hulls to the branches with the no. 0 liner and the sames colors.

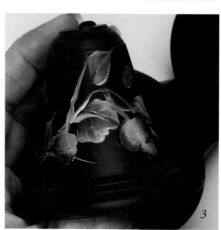

5. *Bell #2 — Individual Strawberries.* On the next bell, repeat the strawberry motif with individual berries sprinkled around the bell. Paint each berry the same as you did in Steps 2 and 3 above, using a no. 10 flat.

6. *Seeds and Hulls.* Finish the individual berries with seeds and hulls. Load Fresh Foliage and a touch of Thicket on an 8/0 liner and dot on the seeds. Paint the hulls with the same colors on a no. 2 flat. Add a tendril here and there if you wish.

Blueberries

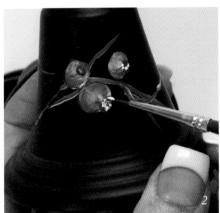

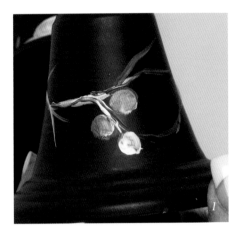

1. Bell #3—Blueberry Vine. Load a no. 2 script liner with Burnt Umber and stroke through Wicker White. Paint a wandering vine and branches around the third bell. Basecoat each blueberry first with Wicker White to help the blue color pop off the black background. Load a no. 2 flat with Cobalt Blue and paint the blueberries.

2. Blossom End. Load a no. 1 script liner with Cobalt Blue and dot dark blue on the blossom end of each berry. Pick up Wicker White and dot around the blue dot for the opening of the blossom end.

3. Leaves. Pull long slender leaves with Fresh Foliage on a no. 2 flat.

4. Bell #4—Individual Blueberries. On the next bell, paint little two- and three-berry clusters. Basecoat each berry with Wicker White. Then paint each berry with two half-circle strokes of Cobalt Blue, allowing the Wicker White to show through in some areas. Load a no. 2 flat with Cobalt Blue and Wicker White and paint the blossom ends.

5. Leaves. Finish with a few little green leaves tucked in between the berries. These long, slender leaves are painted with Fresh Foliage on a no. 2 flat.

Orange Berries

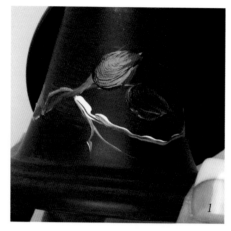

1. Bell #5—Orange Berries and Vine. Load a no. 2 script liner with Burnt Umber and stroke through Wicker White. Paint a wandering vine and branches around the fifth bell. Double load a no. 8 flat with Pure Orange and a little bit of Engine Red and paint the berries the same as you would a one-stroke leaf.

2. Lengthen Tips. With Pure Orange on the no. 8 flat, pull an extended tip on each berry. Fill in with leaves of Fresh Foliage and a little bit of Thicket double loaded on a no. 8 flat.

3. Finish Bell. Add more orange berries around the bell to fill in between the leaves.

4. Bell #6—Individual Orange Berries. On the sixth bell, paint small clusters of orange berries without the brown vine and branches. Double load a no. 8 flat with Pure Orange and a little bit of Engine Red and paint the berries as before. With Pure Orange on the no. 8 flat, pull an extended tip on each berry to elongate them. Tuck a few leaves and stems in among the berries.

Bluebird

1. *Breast and Belly.* The bird's breast and belly are painted with one smooth stroke of School Bus Yellow and Wicker White double loaded on a no. 10 flat.

2. *Head, Wing and Tail.* The head, wing and tail are basecoated with Cobalt Blue and Wicker White double loaded on a no. 10 flat. Shade with Cobalt Blue under the cheek, along the front edge of the wing, and along the top of the tail.

3. *Feathers and Beak.* Layer the feathers by flipping the brush so the Wicker White side is dominant for one layer, then flip the brush again so the Cobalt Blue is dominant for another layer. Paint the beak with School Bus Yellow and Wicker White.

Romantic Floral Swing

Brushes
3/4-inch (19mm) flat
nos. 2, 8 and12 flats
no. 2 script liner

Surface
2-inch x 8-inch (5.1cm x
20.3 cm) pressure treated
board, 24 inches (61cm)
long. Trimmed with stock
chair rail molding on all four
sides. One-inch (25mm)
holes drilled on both sides for
attaching ropes or chains to
suspend from a tree branch.

Additional Supplies
FolkArt Flow Medium

*R*emember when we used to play for hours on the swing, pumping harder and harder to go ever higher? Those swing sets were by necessity plain and utilitarian. Now with durable and weather-proof Outdoor paints and spray finishes, we can bring back those good old days with a romantic and oh-so-pretty swing painted to look like old-fashiond floral chintz fabric. Although this design looks a little complicated, there are really only four different kinds of flowers. I scattered them across the swing seat allowing plenty of the white background to show through.

FOLKART OUTDOOR OPAQUES

| Wicker White | Thicket | Fresh Foliage | Lemon Custard | Pure Orange |

| Purple Lilac | Violet Pansy | Cobalt Blue | Magenta |

1. Basecoat and Vines. Basecoat the entire swing seat with two coats of Wicker White Outdoor Opaque paint. Let dry. Double load Thicket and Fresh Foliage on a no. 12 flat and place the curving vines on the board, starting all of them on the outside edges and working inward toward the center. Lead with the lighter green side of the brush.

2. Large Leaves. With the same brush and colors, pick up some Lemon Custard on the Fresh Foliage side. Paint the larger leaves and pull connecting stems into them from the vines. If your paint starts to grab or drag, dip into Flow Medium when you reload.

3. Dahlia Petals. For the light orange dahlia, double load Pure Orange and Wicker White on a no. 12 flat. Keep picking up fresh Wicker White on your brush as you paint the petals. These are pointed petals on the outside tip—keep the Wicker White on the pointed-tip side. Paint two layers of petals, overlapping the petals of each layer.

4. Third Petal Layer. Paint the next layer of petals using a no. 8 flat. Remember, as your petals get smaller, switch to a smaller brush size.

5. Final Petal Layer. Paint another, smaller layer in the center. If you need yet another layer of petals to fill in the center, pick up more orange on your brush to shade the center.

Lavender and Magenta Flowers

6. *Lavender Flower Petals.* Double-load a no. 8 with Purple Lilac and Wicker White and build the daisy shape of the clusters with little chisel-edge petal strokes.

7. *Petal Layers.* Add another layer of petals to the clusters, picking up Violet Pansy sometimes and Cobalt Blue other times.

8. *Magenta Flowers.* Dot on the lavender flower centers with Lemon Custard. Stroke in the new stems with Fresh Foliage and Lemon Custard on a no. 2 script liner.

The magenta five-petal flowers are painted with a no. 8 flat double loaded with Magenta and Wicker White. These petals have pointed tips. Keep the Magenta to the outside.

9. *Detail Petals.* Load a no. 2 script liner with inky Magenta and draw little detail lines on the petals radiating outward from the centers. Add little chisel-edge buds coming off the sides of the clusters.

10. *Centers.* Dot on the centers with Lemon Custard. Paint the new stems with Fresh Foliage and Lemon Custard on a no. 2 script liner.

11. Blue Flower Petals. Double load Cobalt Blue and Wicker White on a no. 12 flat. Start with five ruffled petals, keeping the Wicker White to the outside. Stroke little buds coming off the main cluster.

12. Yellow Stamens. With a no. 2 script liner, stroke across a puddle of Lemon Custard on your palette and paint the yellow stamen lines that radiate outward from the center.

13. Pollen Dots. Dot on the yellow pollen at the tips of the stamens and shade the centers with a C-stroke of Thicket on a no. 2 script liner.

14. Filler Leaves. When you're finished painting all the flowers on the swing, fill in any empty spaces around and between the flowers with clusters of small one-stroke leaves painted with a no. 2 flat and Fresh Foliage. Pull little stems into them with inky Thicket on a no. 2 script liner.

Blue and Green Trim Lines

15. Blue Trim Line. Accent the top molding on all four sides of the swing seat with Cobalt Blue thinned with Flow Medium.

16. Green Trim Line. Accent the bottom molding on all four sides with Fresh Foliage thinned with Flow Medium if needed.

Ask Donna

Q: What are some other subjects that could be painted on outdoor surfaces besides the ones in this book?

A: The ideas in this book are a drop in the bucket when it comes to designs to paint. What kinds of things do you have in your yard that could use a little sprucing up? Got a birdbath? Greet the arriving bathers with a few painted birds, insects or fish in the bowl of the birdbath. How does your front gate look? As long as it isn't made of chain link or wrought iron and it has a flat surface that can be painted, greet your guests with a flowering vine that always looks fresh. Are you going to have a picnic? Paint some whimsical ants helping themselves to the food right on the picnic table. Instant conversation piece!

When it comes to painting, once you learn how to load your brush and control the movement, the world will become your canvas. Just make sure you don't paint anything that belongs to someone else without getting their permission. I didn't think of that when I painted some of my neighbors' mailboxes. Luckily for me, they loved them!

Gallery of Garden Décor Ideas

The painted designs you have seen in the projects in this book can also be used on just about any surface you may already have in your home. In this section I have taken some of the designs from the previous projects and painted them on such easy-to-find pieces as vases—both clear glass and ceramic, a round metal tray, a tall tin pitcher and a group of colorful citronella candles in little metal buckets. Look around your house and I'll bet you will find all sorts of items that can be turned into eye-catching decorative accessories for your yard or garden, with just a little paint and your own creative touch!

Blue Five-Petal Flowers. This floral design is also painted on one of the porch pillows shown on page 80. The step-by-step painting instructions for these flowers are on pages 84-85. Since this is a glass surface, be sure to use Enamels paints and brushes. Clean the glass first with rubbing alcohol to remove any fingerprints.

Circle of Mixed Flowers. The flowers in this design are the same ones painted individually on the frosted glass candle holders shown in the "Evening Lights" project. See pages 74-79 for step-by-step painting instructions. On this enameled white metal tray, I arranged the flowers and stems to weave a loose circular wreath shape. If you wish, you can place the painted glass candle holders in the center of the tray and use the whole set as a beautiful centerpiece on your outdoor dining table.

Easy Wildflowers. During the summer you can find citronella candles in little metal pails like these at craft stores and discount stores. I found these at Target. Don't you just love the colors? The wildflowers are the same ones I painted on the green metal planter shown on pages 86-89.

Palms on Ceramic Vase. This design picks up on the tropical foliage painted on the Outdoor Beverage Cabinet on pages 50-53. I used the same colors: Butter Pecan, Inca Gold Metallic and Wicker White. Since this is a nonporous ceramic surface, use the Enamels paints and brushes.

Comma Strokes. I found this old-fashioned tin pitcher at a craft store. To give it an elegant, traditional look, I painted it with some nested comma strokes and scrolls. Load a no. 8 round Enamels brush with Metallic Pure Gold Outdoor paint. Sideload into Thicket to shade a few of the comma strokes.

Terra Cotta Wall Planter. Here is a slightly smaller version of the terra cotta wall planter demonstrated on pages 98-103. On this planter, I made the flowers and foliage a little more whimsical and stylized, and I used Outdoor Dimensional paint to accent the design and give it more texture.

Resources

Index

U.S. RETAILERS

PLAID ENTERPRISES, INC.
3225 Westech Dr.
Norcross, GA 30092
Phone: 678-291-8100
www.plaidonline.com

DEWBERRY DESIGNS, INC.
355 Citrus Tower Blvd., Ste. 104
Clermont, FL 34711
Phone: 352-394-7344
www.onestroke.com

DIP 'N ETCH BY ETCHALL
B&B Products, Inc.
19721 N. 98th Ave.
Peoria, AZ 85382
Phone: 623-933-4567
www.etchall.com

WALNUT HOLLOW WOODCRAFT
1409 State Road 23
Dodgeville, WI 53533
Phone: 1-800-950-5101

FREDRIX CANVAS
Tara Materials Inc.
Phone: 1-800-249-8129
www.fredrixartistcanvas.com

CANADIAN RETAILERS

CRAFTS CANADA
120 North Archibald St.
Thunder Bay, ON P7C 3X8
Tel: 888-482-5978
www.craftscanada.ca

FOLK ART ENTERPRISES
P.O. Box 1088
Ridgetown, ON, N0P 2C0
Tel: 800-265-9434

MACPHERSON ARTS & CRAFTS
91 Queen St. E., P.O. Box 1810
St. Mary's, ON, N4X 1C2
Tel: 800-238-6663
www.macphersoncrafts.com

U.K. RETAILERS

CRAFTS WORLD (HEAD OFFICE)
No. 8 North Street
Guildford
Surrey GU1 4 AF
07000 757070

GREEN & STONE
259 Kings Road
London SW3 5EL
020 7352 0837
www.greenandstone.com

HELP DESK
HobbyCraft Superstore
The Peel Centre
St. Ann Way
Gloucester
Gloucestershire GL1 5SF
01452 424999
www.hobbycraft.co.uk

Acorns, 39
Acrylic paints, 8
Address signs, four-season, 32-41
Angular brushes, 10
    double-loading, 13
Anthers, 37, 47
Autumn designs
    address sign, 38-39
    maple leaves, 18

Banana leaves, 52
Basket, 66-67, 70-71
Beach, 56
Berries, 103-109
Birds
    bluebird, 109
    sparrow, 64-65
Blossom, squash, 75
Blueberries, 107
Bluebird, 109
Border
    comma stroke, 103
    leaves, 85
Branches, 38, 62
Brush caddy, 9
Brushes, 10-11
    loading, 12-15
    for paper, painting on
        fabric with, 80-85
    recommended, 96
    rolling, 48
    using handle for dots, 30
Brushes, flipping
    for color variation, 71, 84, 89
    to create segments, 31
Brushstrokes
    chisel-stroke, 40, 49
    comma, 29, 49, 83, 101, 103
    C-stroke, 48
    daisy petal, 76
    half-circle, 100
    for leaves, 16-19
    for petals, 20-23
    random wiggle, 57
    ruffle-edge, 49
    seashell, 45
    teardrop, 49
    U-stroke, 48
Butterflies, 49, 85
    blue, 29
    orange and yellow, 30
    on pillow, 83
    white, 89
    yellow, 44-46
Butterfly houses, 42-49

Cabinet, 50-53
Canvas, stretched, 9, 54-59

Carousel, double-loading, 9
Ceramics brushes, 11
Chisel-edge strokes, 21, 41, 40, 49, 76, 77, 84
Clock, 60-65
Clouds, 56
Color recipe cards, 121-128
Color variation, 52-53, 71
Comma strokes, 29, 49, 101
    border, 103
    long and short, 83
Coneflower, pink, 76
C-stroke
    layered leaf, 16
    for rose, 48

Dahlia, 112
Daisy, lavender, 35
Daisy petal stroke, 20, 76
Daylilies, 47, 78, 94-97
Design, penciling in, 100
Dimensional paint, 35, 37, 46, 47, 58
    outlining with, 35, 46, 96
    for tendrils and spirals, 69
Dip 'n Etch, 73-74
Dots
    pollen, 114
    using brush handle
        for, 30
Double-loading
    angular brush, 13
    to create leaf segments, 52
    filbert brush, 14
    flat brush, 12
    scruffy brush, 14
    sponge painter, 15, 47
Double-loading carousel, 9
Dragonflies, 31, 93
Drinking glasses, 72-79

Enameled metal, 86-89, 90-93, 116
Enamel paints, 8
EtchAll Dip 'n Etch, 73-74
Eye, bird, 65

Fabric, for pillow, 80-85
Fabric liner, for basket, 66-67, 70-71
Fan brushes, 10
    multi-loading, 15
Feathers, 64-65, 109
Ferns, 83, 84, 92-93
Filbert brushes, 10
    double-loading, 14
Five-petal flowers
    layered, 22, 47, 69, 71
    ruffled, 58, 75
Flat brushes, 10

double-loading, 12
multi-loading, 14
sideloading, 13
Float, sideload, 13
Flowers
    on basket liner, 70-71
    centers, 35, 76
    coneflower, 76
    dahlia, 112
    daisies, 20, 35
    daylilies, 78, 94-97
    five-petal layered, 22, 47,
      69, 71
    on gardening gloves, 68
    hydrangeas, 22
    inspiration for, 62
    lavender, 77, 113
    lilies, 23
    magenta, 89, 113
    magnolias, 60-65
    pansies, 44-46
    petals, 20-23
    on pillow, 84-85
    purple, 48-49
    roses, 34, 48-49, 77, 98-
      103, 117
    squash blossom, 75
    on straw hat, 69
    tiger lily, 36
    tropical, 58-59
    trumpet, 88
    tulips, 21, 34-35
    wildflower, 79
    See also Leaves, Petals,
      Stamens
Flowers, blue, 114
    and magenta, 89
    and orange daylilies, 47
Foliage, background, 57
Fronds, 92
Frosting glasses, 73-74

Gardening gloves, 66-68
Garden insect stakes, 26-31
Glass brushes, 11
Glasses, 72-79
Gloves, brushed leather,
    66-68
Grasses, 19

Hairlines, on petals, 45
Hat, straw, 66-67, 69
Head, bird, 64, 109
Heart shapes, making acorns
    from, 39
Highlighting, 101
Hulls, 106
Hydrangea petal, pointed,
    22

Insects
    butterflies, 29-30, 44-46,
      49, 89, 85, 89
    dragonflies, 31, 93
    garden stakes, 26-31

Jagged-edge petal, 21

Lacquer, 101
Ladybug, 28
Landscape, tropical, 54-59
Lavender, 77, 113
Layering, for pine cone seg-
    ments, 40
Leaf clusters, 82
Leather, brushed, 66-68
Leaves
    autumn, 38
    banana, 52
    blue, 82
    blueberry, 107
    dahlia, 112
    daylilies, 47
    details, 71
    fern, 83
    filler, 39, 114
    foreground, 58
    large, 84
    long and slender, 16, 53,
      79, 88
    one-stroke, 68, 69, 89
    rose, 102
    and stems, 44, 48
    techniques for painting,
      16-19
    wide, 93
    See also Palm fronds, Pine
      needles
Lilies
    daylilies, 47, 78, 94-97
    tiger, 36-37
Lily petal stroke, 23
Liner. See Script liner
Loading, 12-15

Magnolias, 60-65
Mailbox, 90-93
Maple leaf, autumnal, 18
Materials and supplies, 8-11
Mediums, 9
Metal surfaces
    mailbox, 90-93
    pails, 116-117
    planter, 86-89
    tray, 116
    wind chimes, 104-109
Multi-loading
    fan brush, 15
    flat brush, 14

Numbers, stenciled or free-
    hand, 34, 37, 38, 40

One-stroke leaves, 16, 68, 82
Orange berries, 108
Outdoor painting, recom-
    mended paints and
    brushes, 96
Outdoor paints, 8
Outlining
    with dimensional paint,
      35, 46, 96
    with script liner, 28, 31,
      36, 102

Pails, metal, 116
Paint, 8, 96
    inky, loading script liner
      with, 15
    making transparent, 29
Painting supplies, 9
Palette, 9
Palm fronds, 19, 53
Palm trees, 57-58
Pansies, 44-46
Paper, brushes for, 11, 80-85
Petals
    chisel-edge, 77
    drooping, 63
    magnolia, 62-64
    outlining, 35
    pointed, 78, 96
    techniques for painting,
      20-23
    turned-edge, 63
Pillows, 80-85
Pine cones, 40
Pine needles, 40
Pitcher, 117
Planters, 86-89, 98-103
Pots, paintings of, 92
Pouncing, 76

Rake brushes, 10
Resources, 118
Roses
    lavender, 34
    pink, 48-49
    stylized, 98-103, 117
    versatility of, 77
    yellow, 34
Round brushes, 11
Ruffle-edge strokes, 23, 49,
    58-59, 75, 88

Sand, 57
Script liner, 11
    loading, with inky paint,
      15
    outlining with, 28, 31

shading with, 35, 37,
    39, 41
Scruffy brushes, 10-11
    double-loading, 14
Seashell strokes, 21, 45
Seeds, strawberry, 106
Shading, 39, 93, 97, 100
    with script liner, 35, 37,
      39, 41
Sideload float, 13
Sideloading, flat brush, 13
Signs, address, 32-41
Sky, 56
Snow, detailing, 41
Sparrow, 64-65
Spattering, 57
Spirals, 69
Sponge painters, 9
    double-loading, 15, 47
    for landscape, 56
Spring address sign, 34-35
Squash blossom, 75
Stamens, 59, 78, 96, 114
Stems, 88
    branching, 75
    chisel-edge, 76
    curving, 77
    fern, 83, 84
    re-stroking, 93
    slender, 89
    stemlets, 79
Strawberries, 106
Straw hat, 66-67, 69
Stripes, 92
Summer address sign, 36-37
Surfaces
    alternate, 46
    cabinet, 50-53
    clock, 60-65
    enameled metal, 86-89,
      90-93, 116
    fabric liner, 66-67, 70-71
    gardening gloves, 66-68
    glass, 72-79
    old, giving new life to, 88
    other ideas for, 115-117
    pillows, 80-85
    straw hat, 66-67, 69
    stretched canvas, 54-59
    terra cotta wall planters,
      98-103
Surfaces, metal
    mailbox, 90-93
    pails, 116-117
    planter, 86-89,
    tray, 116
    wind chimes, 104-109
Surfaces, wooden
    butterfly houses, 42-49
    insect cutouts, 26-31

plaques, 32-41
swing, 110-115
windowbox, 94-97
Swing, wooden, 110-115

Tail, bird, 65, 109
Teardrop stroke, 49
Tear-out color recipe cards,
    121-128
Tendrils, 69
Terra cotta, protecting from
    elements, 101
Terra cotta wall planters,
    98-103, 117
Texture, rough, 57
Tiger lily, 36
Tool container, mailbox as,
    90-93
Trailing flower petals, 23
Tray, 116
Trim, 115
Trumpet flowers, 88
Tulips, 21, 34-35
Turned-edge petal, 63

U-stroke, for rose, 48

Vase designs, 116-117
Vein lines, 30, 85, 96-97
Vine, 70-71, 102
    blueberry, 107
    dahlia, 112
    strawberry, 106
Votive candle holders, 72-79

Wall planters, 98-103, 117
Water, 56
Waves, 57
Wiggle strokes
    leaves, 17, 47
    random, 57
    tulip petals, 21
Wildflower, blue, 79
Wind chimes, 104-109
Windowbox, 94-97
Wings
    bird, 65, 109
    butterfly, 83
Winter address sign, 40-41
Wooden surfaces
    butterfly houses, 42-49
    insect cutouts, 26-31
    plaques, 32-41
    swing, 110-115
    windowbox, 94-97

The best in painting instruction and inspiration is from North Light Books!

Donna Dewberry's ALL NEW Book of One-Stroke Painting

This is the biggest, most complete guide ever to one-stroke painting! Donna Dewberry's popular, proven one-stroke technique—which lets you color, shade and highlight in a single brushstroke—is a cinch to learn, even if you've never picked up a brush before. This must-have resource features over 200 color photos clearly illustrating every detail of Donna's technique; 12 all-new step-by-step projects for painting on tiles, glassware, floorcloths, cabinets, candles, and more; 5 brand new painting techniques that take you beyond one-stroke; and Donna's foolproof advice for creating attractive designs.
ISBN-13: 978-1-58180-706-6, ISBN-10: 1-58180-706-6, Paperback, 160 pages, #33372

Donna Dewberry's Designs for Entertaining

Make your home look festive and inviting for every occasion with *Donna Dewberry's Designs for Entertaining*. This inspiring guide blends more than 60 easy, one-stroke painting projects with fabulous decorating ideas and spectacular table settings. From trays and glassware to tablecloths and candleholders, Donna lends her popular painting style to a range of surfaces, and even shares her own special recipes and party tips. You'll learn step-by-step how to paint on everyday dinnerware, party plates, and even crystal stemware for those extra-special occasions!
ISBN-13: 978-1-58180-799-8, ISBN-10: 1-58180-799-6, Paperback, 160 pages, #33477

The Brushstroke Handbook

The Brushstroke Handbook is your complete reference for mastering more than 50 fabulous strokes using both round and flat brushes. In hundreds of clear and colorful photos, master decorative artist and teacher Maureen McNaughton breaks each stroke down into small movements so you can perfect your brushwork with ease. You'll see how to combine strokes to create gorgeous flowers, birds, butterflies, lace, ribbons and more. Bonus sections on painting fresh and pretty borders plus six lovely compositions put your newfound expertise to work. The lay-flat spiral binding makes it easy to flip through and find the brushstroke you want—instantly!
ISBN-13: 978-1-58180-782-0, ISBN-10: 1-58180-782-1, Hardcover, 144 pages, #33451

Fantastic Floorcloths You Can Paint in a Day

Want to refresh your home décor without the time and expense of redecorating? Then painting canvas floorcloths is for you! Choose from 23 projects simple enough to create in a few hours. Popular decorative painters Judy Diephouse and Lynne Deptula show you step by step how to paint designs ranging from florals to graphic patterns to holiday motifs, including some especially appropriate for kids' rooms. 12 accessory ideas inspire you to create a coordinated look. *Fantastic Floorcloths You Can Paint in a Day* makes home decorating as easy as picking up a paintbrush.
ISBN-13: 978-1-58180-603-8, ISBN-10: 1-58180-603-5, Paperback, 128 pages, #33161

These books and other fine North Light titles are available at your local arts & crafts retailer, bookstore, or from online suppliers.

Color Recipe Cards

Have you ever made a trip to the craft or art supply store to buy paints for the projects you want to do, then forgotten which colors you need? Here's the answer to that problem!

On this and the next seven pages are photos of all the projects in this book. On the back of each photo is a "Color Recipe Card" showing all the colors you will need to paint each project. These cards are already perforated so you can easily tear out the ones you need and take them with you to the store. If you cannot find the same brand of paint, the color swatches on the cards will make it easy to match the colors I used to other brands as closely as possible.

When you are finished with your card, just store it in the handy pocket on the inside back cover of this book. Now shopping for new paint colors is quick, easy and fun!

Four-Season Address Signs

PLAID FOLKART OUTDOOR OPAQUES

Fresh Foliage   Yellow Ochre   Magenta   Wicker White   Purple Lilac

School Bus Yellow   Thicket   Light Blue   Pure Orange   Berry Wine

Engine Red   Burnt Umber   Cobalt Blue

PLAID FOLKART OUTDOOR DIMENSIONALS

Fresh Foliage   Wicker White   Lemon Custard

Butterfly Houses

PLAID FOLKART OUTDOOR OPAQUES

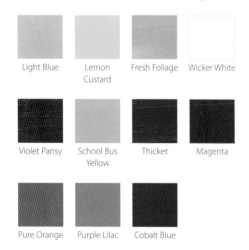

Light Blue   Lemon Custard   Fresh Foliage   Wicker White

Violet Pansy   School Bus Yellow   Thicket   Magenta

Pure Orange   Purple Lilac   Cobalt Blue

PLAID FOLKART OUTDOOR DIMENSIONALS

Fresh Foliage   Wicker White   Lemon Custard

Garden Insect Stakes

PLAID FOLKART OUTDOOR OPAQUES

Engine Red   Berry Wine   Licorice   Wicker White

Cobalt Blue   School Bus Yellow   Lemon Custard

PLAID FOLKART OUTDOOR METALLICS

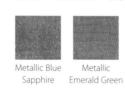

Metallic Blue Sapphire   Metallic Emerald Green

At the Beach

PLAID FOLKART OUTDOOR OPAQUES

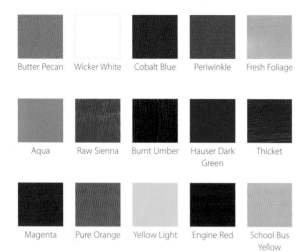

Butter Pecan	Wicker White	Cobalt Blue	Periwinkle	Fresh Foliage
Aqua	Raw Sienna	Burnt Umber	Hauser Dark Green	Thicket
Magenta	Pure Orange	Yellow Light	Engine Red	School Bus Yellow

PLAID FOLKART OUTDOOR DIMENSIONALS

Lemon Custard	Fresh Foliage

Outdoor Beverage Cabinet

PLAID FOLKART OUTDOOR OPAQUES

Butter Pecan	Wicker White

PLAID FOLKART OUTDOOR METALLICS

Inca Gold Metallic

For the Gardener

PLAID FOLKART OUTDOOR OPAQUES

Pure Orange	Engine Red	Cobalt Blue	Wicker White
Green Forest	Fresh Foliage	Yellow Light	

PLAID FOLKART OUTDOOR DIMENSIONALS

Fresh Foliage	Lemon Custard

Magnolias Outdoor Clock

PLAID FOLKART ACRYLICS

Burnt Umber	Wicker White	Berry Wine

Garden Tools Mailbox

PLAID FOLKART OUTDOOR OPAQUES

| Soft Apple | Yellow Ochre | Lemon Custard | Wicker White | Engine Red |

| Thicket | Fresh Foliage | Barn Wood |

PLAID FOLKART OUTDOOR METALLICS

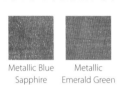

| Metallic Blue Sapphire | Metallic Emerald Green |

Evening Lights

PLAID FOLKART ENAMELS

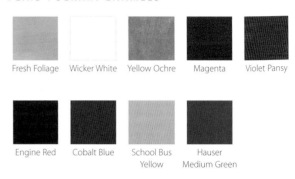

| Fresh Foliage | Wicker White | Yellow Ochre | Magenta | Violet Pansy |

| Engine Red | Cobalt Blue | School Bus Yellow | Hauser Medium Green |

Windowbox with Daylilies

PLAID FOLKART OUTDOOR OPAQUES

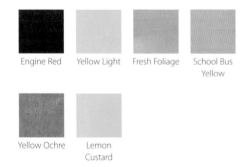

| Engine Red | Yellow Light | Fresh Foliage | School Bus Yellow |

| Yellow Ochre | Lemon Custard |

PLAID FOLKART OUTDOOR DIMENSIONALS

| Fresh Foliage | Lemon Custard |

Romantic Floral Swing

PLAID FOLKART OUTDOOR OPAQUES

| Fresh Foliage | Wicker White | Thicket | Lemon Custard | Pure Orange |

| Purple Lilac | Cobalt Blue | Magenta | Violet Pansy |

Garden Tools Mailbox

PLAID FOLKART OUTDOOR OPAQUES

Soft Apple   Yellow Ochre   Lemon Custard   Wicker White   Engine Red

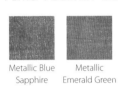

Thicket   Fresh Foliage   Barn Wood

PLAID FOLKART OUTDOOR METALLICS

Metallic Blue Sapphire   Metallic Emerald Green

Evening Lights

PLAID FOLKART ENAMELS

Fresh Foliage   Wicker White   Yellow Ochre   Magenta   Violet Pansy

Engine Red   Cobalt Blue   School Bus Yellow   Hauser Medium Green

Windowbox with Daylilies

PLAID FOLKART OUTDOOR OPAQUES

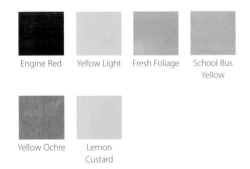

Engine Red   Yellow Light   Fresh Foliage   School Bus Yellow

Yellow Ochre   Lemon Custard

PLAID FOLKART OUTDOOR DIMENSIONALS

Fresh Foliage   Lemon Custard

Romantic Floral Swing

PLAID FOLKART OUTDOOR OPAQUES

Fresh Foliage   Wicker White   Thicket   Lemon Custard   Pure Orange

Purple Lilac   Cobalt Blue   Magenta   Violet Pansy

Wildflower Planter

PLAID FOLKART ENAMELS

Fresh Foliage   Thicket   Pure Orange   Wicker White

Cobalt Blue   Magenta

Pillows for the Porch

PLAID FOLKART ACRYLICS

Cobalt Blue   Wicker White   Thicket   Yellow Light

Fresh Foliage   Yellow Ochre

Berry Pretty Wind Chimes

PLAID FOLKART OUTDOOR OPAQUES

Burnt Umber   Wicker White   Fresh Foliage   Thicket   Pure Orange

Engine Red   Cobalt Blue   School Bus Yellow

Terra Cotta Wall Planters

PLAID FOLKART OUTDOOR OPAQUES

Pure Orange   Engine Red   Burnt Umber   Berry Wine   Fresh Foliage

Thicket   Wicker White   School Bus Yellow   Yellow Ochre